FRENCH ACHIEVEMENT
IN LITERATURE

FRENCH ACHIEVEMENT IN LITERATURE

WILL G. MOORE

Fellow and Tutor of
St. John's College, Oxford

LONDON
G. BELL AND SONS, LTD

SBN 7135 1508 2

Printed in Great Britain by
NEILL & CO. LTD., EDINBURGH

CONTENTS

Foreword

I HOPE THAT the curious arrangement of material in this book may prove helpful rather than irritating, but you never know. The book arose from a course of extra-mural lectures, which attempted to present from a somewhat new angle the rather hackneyed subject known in some circles as French literature. For a modern audience of non-experts, many of the assumptions of the textbooks do not count, and the apparatus of learning hides the matter. People who are skilled in other fields do not wish to know what has been written about literature, they want literature. In other words, they wish to make contact with the great books, not with books about books. (Anyone who knows the bookstore of an American university will recall an amusing proliferation of both kinds of writing). Since literature exists for enjoyment, they wish to enjoy, and can do without discussions of influence, genesis, sources, currents and the rest.

It seemed to me that for once it might be profitable to examine some of the world's literature from this point of

view. One might call it the layman's angle. It might lead
to rediscovery of the variety and scope of a body of
writing with which over the years one had become too
familiar. Suppose that about such a vast literature as the
French one asked the simplest questions. Questions like:
where do the French think they have succeeded best?
What are their best books? How should they be read?
To some these will seem silly questions, but for the
lecturer at least, and I think for the class also, they produced some interesting answers. They showed me that
Anglo-Saxons do not naturally pick out the most
'French' of French books. They do not remember, in
judging a foreign work, for whom it was written and at
what time. If we who teach could remember this, if we
could put ourselves in the intellectual situation of the
author and see what he was aiming at, then we might well
get more out of what he wrote. This in fact happened
to some degree with my audience, and this perhaps is what
extra-mural university work in literature is really meant
to do, to introduce people to great literature and let it
have its way with them. Is not this the opposite of what
happens in much teaching of literature, from A Level
onwards? We set out a syllabus of study, and that means
that students must do the study ... to what end?
Presumably in order to enjoy more fully. Extra-murally
one can reverse the process: allow students to enjoy and
thus give them the incentive to study further if and
where they will.

We started by questioning the usual divisions of
literature and in particular of histories of literature, into
three parts: poetry, drama, fiction. Some of the most
impressive French authors do not fit into this strait-
jacket. At random one thinks of Montaigne, Pascal, La

Rochefoucauld, Péguy. It gave us, as I now think, a useful jolt to see what the French had done in the production of comedy, of essays, of epigrams, of satire, not considering any one genre as more central than the rest. We found ourselves looking at well-known works from a new standpoint. We actually found ourselves studying dictionaries. In fact, to look at what the French have actually *done* in literary production is an exercise full of surprises. One of the surprises was that we found no biographies. French writers seem to have written splendid memoirs, about themselves; they appear to have no Lockhart or Trevelyan. The life of Pascal by his sister seems to be almost an exception. Chateaubriand's life of Rancé and Renan's life of Jesus, both great books, are not biography in any usual sense.

The great omission in the lectures, as in these pages, I feel to be that of all writing previous to 1500. I am too old a teacher to think that one can put a date to 'modern' literature and I could wish that my own competence extended into the medieval field. Since the spirit of much medieval literature is not easily accessible to modern students perhaps there is room for a separate book on the subject.

One difficulty which besets students of French art is that the subject has to be taken out of a sort of cocoon of frivolity. When you say 'French' many people think of risky novels and 'light' literature. Aldous Huxley hit off this point happily in *The Gioconda Smile:*

'French ? I am so fond of French.' Mrs Hutton spoke of the language of Racine as if it had been a dish of green peas.

But we need not fear. Once we have introduced any keen student to any of the greater French writers, to

Racine or to Pascal, or to Diderot or to Gide or to Proust, they exert their own authority. The teacher may, as Rousseau said every teacher should, disappear.

1 *Autobiography*

WHY IS IT THAT Frenchmen have written much and often about themselves and hardly at all about each other? Their literature contains hardly a single notable biography, and it abounds in memoirs. Writers as different in temperament as Commines and Brantôme, for instance, and who both lived in times when there was no sale for a book about oneself, as there is today, yet thought it worth much time and effort to set out for others to read what had happened to them, what they had seen of the world, of the great, of the mysterious working of chance and fate. Commines writes as a statesman, dry, caustic, patient, sceptical. Brantôme seems in comparison to write like a child, to have no important thoughts and no depth of mind. But what an eye for a spectacle, what a pen to describe a scene. He reports chatter and gossip as if they were important, but in describing a tournament or an assassination, he misses no eloquent detail, all is alive, 'close' as Dryden would say. The great occasion, the tense moment, these he will describe without ornament.

5

Schiller, with the eye of genius, thought one such passage worthy of the ballad form:

> Un jour que François Ier s'amusait à regarder un combat de ses lions, une dame ayant laissé tomber son gant dit à De Lorges: si vous voulez que je croie que vous m'aimez autant que vous me le jurez tous les jours, allez ramasser mon gant. De Lorges descend, ramasse le gant au milieu de ces terribles animaux, remonte, le jette au nez de la dame, et depuis, malgré toutes les avances et les agaceries qu'elle lui faisait, ne voulut jamais la voir.

Eight lines, and only one word to suggest the danger (terribles). Yet the short simple phrases convey, as Proust will do, a meeting-point of frivolity and mortality. As we shall see, Mme de La Fayette appreciated this writer, and read him carefully.

A much stronger personality emerges from the memoirs of Retz. Paul de Gondi was made to be a Churchman in an age of civil war. He emerged as a Cardinal but admitted in his book that he was 'l'âme la moins ecclésiastique qui fût dans l'univers' and during the Fronde, that French Civil War so like our own, he played a double role with great skill. Much later, in retirement and disgrace, he wrote a brilliant account of his adventures and intrigues. As we read we find ourselves presented with a sort of primer of revolution; with the greatest candour Retz explains how politicans are forced by events to lie and turn the truth, to be all things to all men, to know the right moment to be brave, and to be cunning. His breathless pages describe a confused and decadent society, the sort of society which explains the maximes of La Rochefoucauld, his enemy and contemporary. For both men, deception is an essential element in politics and what the Church may frown upon may be the royal road to success:

> Les vices d'un archevêque peuvent être, dans une infinité de rencontres, les vertus d'un chef de parti.

Since no participant can know how things will go or how different men are from their speech, the game of politics is the most exciting and hazardous of games; nothing can be done on principle, the empirical is the only way to success. Not for nothing did Gibbon think the memoirs of Retz worth quotation.

We are accustomed to think of the Fronde as the last outburst of the French nobility before submitting to the despotism of Louis XIV. But this is too simple a picture. Modern research has revealed the turbulence that continued in all levels of French life: unrest in the army, in the church, at court, among the middle class and the peasants. This can be read in the memoirs of an aristocrat who was convinced that Louis XIV was a bad ruler. Whether he was right or wrong, Henri Louis de Rouvroy, Duc de Saint-Simon, was certainly a great writer, a writer whose passion and eloquence make the pages even of Retz look dull by comparison. Historians discuss how great was his bias and how reliable his information. But these things need not deter students of literature from enjoying these passionate pages, this apparently unending series of incidents, sketches, conversations (seven volumes in the Pléiade series, and, we are told, much more which has not been published). Some pages are dull; Saint-Simon is not a great mind, his view was narrow, snobbish, old-fashioned. He can indeed be as annoying as Balzac, a writer of comparable imaginative power. Both men excel in conveying in words a graphic vision of people, many people, of conflicting interests, of people under emotion. Both of them cover a wide canvas, nothing less than a *comédie humaine*, and it was their range and power of vision that made Proust see in them his masters. The great figures of the *Mémoires* are monsters of cruelty and duplicity. Surely, we say, Louvois and Mme de Mainte-non cannot have been as bad as they here appear. Some of these portraits make us shiver. Harlay for example, the leading lawyer of his day, brilliant, incisive, formidable on the bench, and in private . . . something very different.

> . . . sans honneur effectif, sans meurs dans le secret, sans probité qu'extérieure, sans humanité même, en un mot, un hypocrite parfait, sans foi, sans loi, sans Dieu et sans âme, cruel mari, père barbare, frère tyran, ami uniquement de soi-même, méchant par nature, se plaisant à insulter, à outrager, à accabler, et n'en ayant de sa vie perdu une occasion.

French has never been written like this, with an apparently inexhaustible succession of little phrases, adding up to an immense indictment. Most impressive is the indictment of the king himself, for his vanity, his ignorance, his obstinacy, his love of power and of money. Extravagance, we feel, cannot go further than what the Sun King spent on his palaces. Marly for instance, intended to be 'a little place' for a few visitors, and which in the end, by changing the landscape, building, painting, altering, furnishing, outran even Versailles in expense. Page after page we read of this kind and then come to the summing up, which has a resonance and a Miltonic finality:

> Voilà où conduit l'aveuglement des choix, l'orgueil de tout faire, la jalousie des anciens ministres et

> capitaines, la vanité d'en choisir de tels qu'on ne put leur rien attribuer, pour ne partager la réputation de grand avec personne . . . enfin toute cette déplorable façon de gouverner qui précipita dans le plus évident péril d'une perte entière, et qui jeta dans le dernier désespoir ce maître de la paix et de la guerre, ce distributeur de couronnes, ce châtieur des nations, ce conquérant, ce grand par excellence, cet homme immortel pour qui on épuisait le marbre et le bronze, pour qui tout était à bout d'encens.

With such a writer every quotation has to be cut off before the end. One feels there need be no end to this immensely detailed vision. And it is not only a question of words. This man either remembers or invents or en- flames the dramatic point, where views and personalities clash, where man is stopped, his will and his power checked and where the human condition seems to be conjured up before us.

If this were all, the neglect of Saint-Simon by students of French would be excusable. But it is far from being all. These descriptions are not personal so much as poetic. In the hands of a master artist the random material of a court calendar is transformed into a picture of human life, in which the physical and the moral seem curiously interdependant. One does not know, says a modern scholar, where the one ends and the other begins. Saint-Simon 'knows how to use the random and idiosyncratic, the unselected, the at times absurdly personal and prejudiced, as points of departure for sudden descents into the depths of human existence.' Those who find this judgment startling should read in *Mimesis* the pages of evidence which Prof. Auerbach brings up in its support. One final extract will perhaps bring home more than explanation can do the power and the modernity of this writing. It is the famous description of the Jesuit Father Tellier, in whom Saint-Simon recognises a most powerful and pitiless man:

> Sa tête et sa santé étaient de fer, sa conduite en était aussi, son naturel cruel et farouche ... il était profondément faux, trompeur, caché sous mille plis et replis ... c'était un homme terrible ...

This man is seen at night, face to face, by candlelight:

> Je le voyais bec à bec entre deux bougies, n'y ayant du tout que la largeur de la table entre deux. J'ai décrit ailleurs son horrible physionomie. Eperdu tout-à-coup par l'ouïe et par la vue, je fus saisi, tandis qu'il parlait, de ce que c'était qu'un jésuite, qui par son néant personnel et avoué ne pouvait rien espérer pour sa famille, ni par son état et par ses voeux pour soi-même, pas même une pomme ni un coup de vin plus que les autres; qui par son âge touchait au moment de rendre compte à Dieu, et qui, de propos délibéré et amené avec grand artifice allait mettre l'Etat et la religion dans la plus terrible combustion, et ouvrir la persécution la plus affreuse pour des questions qui ne lui faisaient rien, et qui ne touchaient que l'honneur de leur école de Molina. Ses profondeurs, les violences qu'il me montra, tout cela me jeta en un tel extase, que tout-à-coup je me pris à lui dire en l'interrompant: 'Mon Pere, quel âge avez-vous?' Son extrême surprise, car je le regardais de tous mes yeux, qui la virent se peindre sur son visage, rappela mes sens. (quoted by Auerbach, *Mimesis*, paperback ed., p. 376).

If we meditate such a passage we need not use superlatives as Saint-Simon was always doing, but we shall come to understand why Proust called his work 'une comédie humaine', admired it as much as he did that of Balzac, and hoped to achieve something of similar grandeur.

There is only one Saint-Simon, but many of his nation have tried to put their experiences into words, with remarkable success. A book devoted to them would have to include Grammont, Casanova, Beaumarchais and many another. If we were distinguishing between autobiography and memoir we should give pride of place to the famous *Confessions* of Rousseau, one of the chief source-books of romanticism. Never before had a writer attempted self-analysis on such a scale, 'une gigantesque entreprise' as Georges May says. Rousseau starts (both his book and his method) from the assumption that every individual is unique: 'Si je ne vaux pas mieux, du moins je suis autre'. He therefore tries to pick out from his life remembered incidents, beginnings, pointers which seem to him to have come to some fulfilment. He thus harks back to Augustine and arrives, as Goethe will arrive, at both *Dichtung* and *Wahrheit*.

In some ways the *Confessions* are not a pleasing book. Here is a judgment upon them from a fairminded scholar who knew them as well as most:

> It is impossible to like Rousseau the man; that is the price of such complete self-revelation as his. The reader feels pity or disgust according to temperament and point of view. But the work remains to be reckoned with; there is the eternal appeal of beauty of form often combined with perfect adaptation to function; far more, there is its permanent quality of stimulus, as a leaven which has leavened so much of nineteenth and twentieth century literature from poets to political thinkers.

B

(L. A. Bisson, *A Short History of French Literature*, p. 92).

Of the strength of the influence here referred to there can be little doubt. We may still feel the fascination of this giant of the Enlightenment, who had no use either for Christianity or for pure reason, but who sought God in reason, God in nature and God in the human conscience. Listen to him describing the germination in his mind of his second *Discours*, on Inequality:

> . . . enfoncé dans la forêt j'y cherchais, j'y trouvais l'image des premiers temps, dont je traçais fièrement l'histoire; je faisais main-basse sur les petits mensonges des hommes; j'osais dévoiler à nu leur nature, suivre le progrès du temps et des choses qui l'ont défigurée, et comparant l'homme de l'homme avec l'homme naturel, leur montrer dans son perfectionnement prétendu la véritable source de ses misères. Mon âme, exaltée par ces contemplations sublimes, s'élevait auprès de la Divinité, et voyant de là mes semblables suivre, dans l'aveugle route de leurs préjugés, celle de leurs erreurs, de leurs malheurs, de leurs crimes, je leur criais d'une faible voix qu'ils ne pouvaient entendre: Insensés, qui vous plaignez sans cesse de la nature, apprenez que tous vos maux vous viennent de vous.
>
> (Ed. Garnier, p. 460).

Has the fascination departed? One has the impression that the *Confessions* no longer appeal, save to students of the past.

Yet one of Rousseau's greatest disciples was to write a masterpiece of autobiography. François Marie René, Comte de Chateaubriand, a pioneer in the revival of both poetry and history, is said to have written all his works

about himself, even a biography like his *Vie de Rancé*.
Vanity is present in them all. But even Sainte-Beuve, the
great enemy, who could not stand the parade and the
arrogance, admits to the charm, to the full sorcery of the
style. Chateaubriand realised that he was born into the
poetry of melancholy:

> Le chagrin est mon élément; je ne me retrouve que
> quand je suis malheureux.

Walking through the park of Chantilly, the trees and even
the rain fill him with the thoughts of mortality and prepare
him for that purple passage on the death of the Duc
d'Enghien.

> Revenant le long des haies à peine tracées, la pluie
> m'a surpris; je me suis réfugié sous un hêtre; ses
> dernières feuilles tombaient comme mes années;
> sa cime se dépouillait comme ma tête; il était marqué
> au tronc d'un cercle rouge, pour être abattu comme
> moi. Rentré à mon auberge, avec une moisson de
> plantes d'automne et dans des dispositions peu
> propres à la joie, je vous raconterai la mort du Duc
> d'Enghien, à la vue des ruines de Chantilly.
>
> (*Mémoires d'Outre-tombe*. II. 136).

As contrast, for those who do not like Chateaubriand,
the Journal of the Goncourt brothers seems less pretentious. It notes incidents, attitudes, atmosphere with a
minimum of advertisement but the final picture is immense and impressive, the picture of French society
under the Second Empire. Those nineteen years (1851–70)
which have been called a 'show', in which French politics
seemed even more catastrophic than usual but in which
men of talent were to be found in every sphere. The state
might fall in ruins before Bismarck's armies but

Goncourt and Flaubert and Taine and Maupassant made beautiful work from what all could see to be social collapse.

There is no space to mention the twentieth-century cult of autobiographical writing, pursued in more than one form. Writers who kept no journal have left letters which are often an intellectual piece of autobiography. Gide, the master of the genre, has done both, more than that he has made his works out of his own verifiable experience so that we can follow his development through his art as well as through his letters to Claudel, to Valéry and others. But his journal is possibly the work which is his enduring monument. It is more domestic and personal than other great French memoirs; in some places it seems little more than a day to day account of his reading and his visits. But his style gives form to these and shows him increasingly conscious of what he is really doing:

> Toute notre vie s'emploie à tracer de nous-mêmes un ineffaçable portrait. (Pléiade edition, I. 29).

He claims complete self-revelation but his Journal does not give us this. We know that he tore up hundreds of pages, and moreover, as Enid Starkie found when she talked to him, the more he said the less did he seem to be telling you. The true mastery of style and material in the Journal comes out in his attempts to define his own literary talent. He manages to render articulate that most difficult process whereby he was liberated from a strict protestant frame of life and accepted a freedom which many have thought disastrous:

> Alors, cessant d'appeler tentations mes désirs, cessant d'y résister, je m'efforçais tout au contraire de les suivre . . . L'abandon de soi m'apparut comme

une supérieure sagesse . . . J'étais comme un marin abandonnant les rames et qui se confie aux courants; enfin il prend le temps de regarder les rives; tant qu'il ramait il ne regardait pas. Ma volonté, si constamment tendue, retombait à présent sans emploi; j'en ressentis d'abord certaine gêne et puis cela même disparut, se fondit dans le charme infini de vivre et de vivre n'importe comment. Ce fut le long repos après la longue fièvre. (op. cit. I. 44, 1893)

Twelve years later we find this same moral microscope turned on to the sequence of his books:

Quel que soit le livre que j'écris je ne m'y donne jamais tout entier, et le sujet qui me réclame le plus instamment, sitôt après, se développe cependant à l'autre extrémité de moi-même. . . . On ne tracera pas aisément la trajectoire de mon esprit; sa courbe ne se révélera que dans mon style et échappera à plus d'un. Si quelqu'un dans mon dernier écrit pense saisir enfin ma ressemblance, qu'il se détrompe: c'est toujours de mon dernier-né que je suis le plus différent.

This may be sincerity but what it reveals is the opposite of the clarity suggested by the limpid style. The Journal reveals what Germaine Brée thought to be Gide's chief feature, impenetrability: 'l'insaisissable Protée'. It does however tell us something of the power which André Gide has had, and has himself been, in the world of writing and on successive generations of our century. He once approached a kind of definition even of this most elusive quality:

Je prétends donner à ceux qui me liront force, joie, courage, défiance et perspicacité, mais je me garde surtout de leur donner des directions . . . développer à la fois l'esprit critique et l'énergie, ces deux contraires. (op. cit. I. 785, 1924)

Such in uncertain outline is the nature of the literary landscape which the French seem to me to have covered in the way of autobiography. Many who study their literature come to know only plays and poems and novels, but the vitality and charm of these is partly explained by this other kind of writing. In fact the luck of the alphabet has brought us in a first chapter to a vantage point from which certain things about French literary art become clear to us, as it were from the start: the French have trained themselves to analyse and to evaluate experience, to understand what happens to them, and to give adequate expression to their findings.

2 *Comedy*

EVERY READER OF this book will know something of the French taste for comedy. Ever since writing was invented men have exploited that kind of drama of which the three obvious marks have been the representation of ordinary life, the provoking of laughter and the happy ending. The medieval farce, Patelin for instance, did this in its own special way, by providing the pleasure and surprise of seeing intelligence emerge in unlikely places. The *sotie* took the rather different form of using word-play to suggest that folly can be wise and that fools see things hidden from the wise. The Renaissance return to classical comedy insisted on elegance of form and amused its public by disguises and mistaken identity. The comedies of Corneille, which contain more enjoyment than is often thought, gather up traces of all these forms of drama and contrive to hold a mirror up to a society, to portray fashion and those who will not go along with it. The public who could enjoy Corneille's Alidor was ready for Molière's Alceste.

With the theorists, however, comedy had a hard time.

It had to meet the objections of the purists who wanted logical serious drama, and the demands of the moralists who wanted plays to be improving, to have a 'serious' objective, like tragedy. This misunderstanding is not yet a thing of the past. Even Molière, hard pressed by both kinds of critic, was reduced to reviving the adage 'castigat ridendo mores' and to claim that his plays taxed with impiety were really attempts to correct vice. We can see now that his greatness was not in his moral views but in his grasp of human nature and his gift of showing it to its depths. He thus led comedy back to its real path, to the imaginative portrayal of human behaviour, to the comedy of intelligence (such is the happy title of a recent book) meaning two things: the critique of society by intelligence and the critique of intelligence itself as liable to lead us away from nature. Comedy, said Voltaire, perhaps with something of all this in mind, in Molière's hands was a creation of form out of chaos. Taught by Italian actors in the *commedia dell'arte* tradition he discovered means of giving pleasure more elemental and more satisfying than the wit of Corneille. He did not rely on verse alone, though he used it; nor on words alone, though he invented comic designs with words. But he used mime and gesture, his face in fact, to convey with the greatest subtlety the things which we prefer not to convey, impressions of ourselves that we would rather not give. The contrast between the words and the attitude was indeed one of his main sources of comedy. When he started to act comic actors wore masks, to show the particular extravagance they wished to convey. He abandoned the mask for the face, itself a superlative mask and in his case, said a fellow actor, able to convey any emotion that he wished.

These gifts of the actor were put at the service of an imaginative power, the power of imagining situations, often amusing in themselves but which combine to form a critique of society, of its sophistication, of its accepted norms, of its worship of so-called intelligence and in particular of those features which social custom was concerned to conceal, selfishness, desire for profit, vanity, love of reputation. This imaginative power enabled Molière to present and enforce such contrasts as art and not merely as satire. His art is often satiric but there is enjoyment rather than bitterness in it. The marvel is that his exposure of the climbing *bourgeoisie* in Jourdain is so enjoyable; the afflictions of Arnolphe, the crusty bachelor lover, are enjoyable, partly because he has brought them all on himself. Even miserliness and greed are matter of art in Molière. This may be the key to his comic invention.

The school of drama in which Molière was trained enabled him to present to an intelligent public a spectacle of a quite new dramatic kind, in that it excluded emotion. Medieval drama had indeed encouraged people to watch unmoved the horrors of devils and the malice of tricksters. But the Italians managed this with ordinary behaviour. They portrayed fools for whom we feel no pity, and knaves who inspire no fear. This is a presentation of character which English people neither like nor understand. An English audience is not happy with a Tartuffe, unless the plot turns to his defeat. A French audience will not take him so seriously, will see him, not as a person at all but as a sketch, a silhouette. They have indeed no time to see him as a person, since he is always shown at speed and always in contrast, with others, with himself. This may seem to us poor psychology, but its power of suggestion is enormous. As soon as we give up the idea that a dramatic character must be 'real' then we can enjoy the comedy.

Comedy in our usual sense is something amusing but superficial. French classical comedy is as deep as tragedy, by reason of its impersonality. We watch, not people but attitudes, which turn out to be our attitudes. Remarks seem to break loose from their context and to refresh us by their universal application. When Jourdain exults in his discovery that he has been speaking prose for forty years, this tells us nothing about him, as an individual. This is an artistic suggestion about European man. This suggests with grace and freshness an attitude of novelty and naïveté: what is more comic than that, offered to a sophisticated middle class? Alceste's famous line, 'J'ai pour moi la justice, et je perds mon procès' exactly hits off, not an individual called Alceste, but the belief deep in all of us that right should win, and that it is a scandal that innocence should, in the all-too-human justice of the courts, be pronounced guilty.

Molière is not so much nor so frequently a funny writer as he is comic in the French classical sense of perceiving and rendering the unreasonable, alongside the suggestion of its opposite. In a defence of *Tartuffe* (which is anonymous but now taken to be his own) he put his view in a sentence:

> Le ridicule est la forme extérieure et sensible de ce qui manque entièrement de raison.

So we are shown how, in a miser for instance, the love of money is carried to lengths which we naturally regard as absurd and which make this very human miser into something we can hardly call human:

> Le Seigneur Harpagon est, de tous les humains,
> l'humain le moins humain.

Even more remarkably we are shown a fool, George
Dandin, who believes in justice and has not the wit to
get it, which inspires him with the immortal reflexion:

> J'enrage d'avoir tort lorsque j'ai raison.

So do we all. But only a comic poet can find a way of
taking the sting out of the bitterness by putting the
words in the mouth of a man so stupid that, as we say,
'he has only himself to blame'.

It is well known that Molière died almost on the stage,
performing a role in which he had given himself the part
of a man who wished Molière to die: 'that will teach him
to make fun of the Faculty of Medicine.' There is more
than surface irony here. He had imagined in *Le Malade
Imaginaire* what many have taken for satire but something
that goes much deeper. He imagined a man who believed
that the doctor must be right, and that when the doctor
says you are ill, well then, you are ill. He shows experts
who get away with ignorance because they wear learned
clothes and use learned jargon and in their clutches a
superstitious man, who is told to trust nature, to realise
that if he feels well the chances are that he is not ill. A
moving dialogue, not funny in our sense but richly comic
in its suggestions of a society with its values all wrong,
human dignity being threatened by jargon, things being
mixed up with names. Argan is told by the apothecary
that he will, for being disobedient, suffer from a string of
diseases, each with a worse name than the last. And his
brother (as it might be the intelligent part of ourselves)
says to him: 'Et ce qu'il dit, que fait-il à la chose?'

It has been well said that no country can expect to have two Molières in its history. Yet the resonance of Molière's achievement has probably affected the development of comedy in France up to the present. The history of the French light comedy has yet to be written. It would start perhaps with Marivaux, who in play after play charmed audiences more sophisticated than those of the seventeenth century with Molièresque situations and yet made for himself a quite original kind of comedy. With liberal use of disguise he offered perfect contrasts of the language of society and the language of the heart. Since no 'profession' of love was certain, the lover used tricks to find out how matters really stood, change of clothes, of sex, of letters, all these play a part in what one of his best plays called 'le jeu de l'amour et du hasard'. Great fantasy, sense of language and of psychology were skilfully used to give pleasure, amusing rather than searching, but French in its intelligence and speed. Such a light play as *Les Sincères* for instance might almost qualify for a television series on 'Boy meets Girl'. Boy does meet girl and both are induced to confess that they are in love . . . with themselves.

For late eighteenth-century Paris, comedy of a sterner kind was offered, by Beaumarchais. The plot may be absurd but the speed and the skill are both abundant, in the service of a new outspokenness. Not for nothing has the valet of this comedy, Figaro, become one of the world's famous comic figures. Figaro is always up against things, and never at a loss. He has the qualities of Molière's Mascarille and Scapin. Above all he has the new note of middle-class protest against social inequality. One wonders how these plays ever passed the censor, plays in which the aristocracy are shown up, authority is mocked, the Bastille described as the symbol of repression less than ten years before it really became one. As Figaro shows up the absurdity of French class-structure we feel that Molière's valets have taken on new life.

But comedy depends on a social stability for its audience and things were to get worse because of the Revolution. Nobody ever tried to repeat Beaumarchais' tour de force of making comedy a sounding board. Only one of the Romantics succeeded in recovering with any dramatic force the truly comic spirit. The *Comédies et Proverbes* of Alfred de Musset were, despite their early failure, most clever incarnations of Romantic comedy. As in Molière, the old opponents face each other on stage: education versus naïveté, youth versus age, decorum versus spontaneity. Camille and Perdican come to no understanding because they are too well bred. Modern education has made their reactions unnatural. So Perdican flirts with a country girl, to her ruin. Not many comedies contain a death. Did this one get out of hand, or was Musset experimenting with a fantasy which could be brought close to reality? We shall never know, and opinions will always differ; and the play will keep its fascinating secret.

It may be that study of French classical comedy blinds one's sight, but I could not name a comic masterpiece produced by the French within the last hundred years. Comedy seems to invade fiction and opera and to satisfy the boulevard audiences. Anatole France seems to inherit the mantle of Molière more effectively than Feydeau or Labiche or Jules Romains or Courteline. If this were a lengthy book we could find in Giraudoux and in Cocteau a truly modern fantasy, perhaps a comic view of life, but it is not obvious, not plain for all to see. Perhaps, as

Meredith said in an essay which has not yet lost its sting, comedy depends for success on a sophisticated and socially stable audience. It is not an art for troubled times.

3 Dictionary

MANY PEOPLE WOULD not consider a dictionary to be a work of literature. Having no form, no arrangement, save that of the alphabet it would seem a vehicle neither for art nor for ideas. Yet the French have produced at least three dictionaries which have not only influenced literature but which may claim to be themselves works of literature. And among these I do not count Voltaire's inspired little book to which he gave the title of *Dictionnaire Philosophique Portatif*, which is no true dictionary but an alphabetical listing of discussion points, in order to get them across quickly without subordinating any to the rest.

Of the three dictionaries I speak of here, the least important (as literature) is the most scientific. It must surely count among the great dictionaries of the world, its title *Dictionnaire de la Langue Française*, compiled by Emile Littré in the decade preceding the Franco-German war. It is a remarkable thing that no major writer since that time (Goncourt, Renan, Proust, France, Gide, Valéry) has any place in the most authoritative of French dictionaries. The exclusions of Littré therefore reflect its horizons, not only in time but in outlook. The language has changed considerably since 1872 but Littré has no established successor.

Littré codified and gave fresh life to educated usage of 1870. One could not say that he induced his readers to take a fresh view of the world. But this is just what could be said of both Bayle and Diderot. Until recently neither counted among the major French authors. The second has now been studied and celebrated; some work has been done on the first, but I wonder whether his merits as a pioneer of the Age of Enlightenment have been properly appreciated.

Achieved almost single-handed, the *Dictionnaire Historique et Critique* of Pierre Bayle (published in 1696, revised in 1702 and 1730) is a marvel of industry and persistence. In an age of orthodoxy and hierarchy, when the authority of the Church was such that no effective critique of its pronouncements was possible, Bayle set out to defend a principle for which many of his fellow Protestants had died, the right of private judgment. He set out to see for himself how far the facts supported the official version. His enormous reading, no less than his position at the heart of cross-currents of new ideas in Rotterdam, allowed him to present differing views on biblical figures, church fathers, historical characters. Some say that he delighted to show the Church was wrong, for example in thinking of King David as an admirable character. This is hardly fair. Bayle was not concerned to win, in that sense. He was passionately concerned to keep assertion under the control of known fact, and to point out where assertions went beyond known facts or selected the known facts. This, at the start of the 18th century, was a service not only to learning and to truth, but to the development of ideas. More than on any particular point, Bayle wins by suggesting a new attitude to history, an attitude of reserve, of admission that very much is and must remain unknown. Since we can never know how things in the past actually happened, we should beware of those who claim to know what supports their view.

It is no wonder that among a nation so naturally critical as the French such a book as Bayle's Dictionary had enormous success and influence. Despite its formidable weight and size—three quarto volumes—it must have been read by most writers of the 18th century, and we may say that it helped to bring about an entire revolution in the way a thinking person looked at the past. We can see its effect if we compare the world of Bossuet with that of Montesquieu. Both enquire into ancient times, both were learned men. But Bossuet knows what happened. He has entire confidence in the Bible as history. Montesquieu is in another world, in a world full of uncertainty, in which the Bible is a local, biassed, limited book. On all sorts of questions Bossuet has a clear answer, inspired by the Bible. Montesquieu has no answer, but is asking new questions, which have led by trial and error to the modern view of history. No wonder that such a Dictionary was a favourite book of Voltaire. It is said that Frederick the Great had a copy of the Dictionary placed before him when he staged a parody of a trial for heresy.

One would think such a book as Bayle's Dictionary was hardly a book and hardly readable. Strangely enough this is not the case. Pick it up where you will, you will find it absorbing, and will soon get used to the complicated

C

arrangement of a text in large print, notes to the text, often much more voluminous than the text, in closer print, and references, in still smaller print, down the margins. Books which Bossuet tried to suppress, such as Richard Simon's critical histories of the books of the Old and New Testaments, are quoted by Bayle. His range is enormous, including Augustine and Spinoza, Pythagoras and Rorarius, this last as a source for the view that animals can reason, and therefore of use to Bayle in opposing Descartes, whose ideas he submits to criticism as relentless as anything from the Bible. The article on King David raised more stir perhaps than any other, for Bayle had to avoid the official view of the king as saint and psalmist but he had also to by-pass acute differences of opinion within Protestant circles.

Why is Bayle's Dictionary different from other dictionaries? I think because he was the first man who made a dictionary into a weapon, not just to defend his own views but to bring new evidence to bear on all views, to make people think what it means to have a view at all, what it means to say you accept a fact, that you believe in a way of thinking or of living. It is no accident that this new kind of dictionary appears at the same time as the Church in Europe is split by increasing and apparently endless quarrels, all about one thing, as to who is right. Jansenists, Jesuits, Calvinists, Arminians, Protestants, Catholics, Quietists, Gallicans . . . these were only some of the parties who were concerned that their 'truth' should prevail, that the 'truth' of the Bible should support their cause and refute their enemies. This is the end of a long process which began before the Reformation. The heresies which split the medieval Church we may see as the first stirrings of a movement of enquiry which

by 1700 had reached tragic proportions. One of its most
spectacular scandals was the great duel between Bossuet
and Fénelon, which reduced two of the ablest men of the
age to a war of words which became a struggle of
intrigue, where in Rome each had his agents, each was
forced to employ all sorts of means to secure the Pope's
verdict for his view. All this is the background to the
liberating work (as it now appears) of men like Fontenelle
and Bayle, Montesquieu and Voltaire. It was not a
question of such men being quarrelsome or awkward; it
was really a question of what one should believe, and
how one should interpret the past. In the painful
elaboration of the modern view I know no more effective
document than Bayle's Dictionary.

Bayle once said that he had to play two parts at once:

> Il a fallu que dans cet amas de toutes sortes de
> matières je soutinsse deux personnages, celui
> d'historien et celui de commentateur.
> (*Pierre Bayle*, Choix de textes, ed. Raymond, 1948,
> p. 41).

I take him to mean that he had not only to find things out,
to check, clarify, sort out, what biassed authorities had
reproduced in their own way and to further their own
cause. He had to judge what they said, to apply to the
facts a critical intelligence. If we wish to get some idea
of the enormous scale on which he attempted this we have
only to take the first volume of any early edition of the
Dictionary, and go through the nine packed pages which
are simply a list of the articles we shall find. Here is a
sample, the start of the letter R:

> Racan, Radziwil, Raimarus, Raynand, Ramus, Ran-
> gouge, Raphelengius, Rapin. . . .

Such a task is appalling in its demands on courage and on human physique. Bayle's Dictionary is one of the wonders of literature. But not only for its bulk. It is paradoxically an original book, even though it consists only of facts taken from others and of arguments for and against what others have argued. For the first time we find in this man the modern attitude to history. Until this time history was just the facts about the past. Even Pascal, great scientist as he was, had no conception of what we call the science of history. For him it was a science of memory: one had to know what Caesar, for instance, said and did; one's judgment was not involved. We do not now think so. Bayle seems to have been one of the first to stop thinking in this way, the first to have realised the now hackneyed fact that what happened is mostly unattainable, lost in the mists of time. All we can do is to recover what someone said or did as a result of what happened. He is worth hearing on this point:

> Je vous avoue que je ne lis presque jamais les historiens dans la vue de m'instruire des choses qui se sont passées, mais seulement pour savoir ce que l'on dit dans chaque nation et dans chaque parti sur les choses qui se sont passées.

If we put this beside what Bayle's comrade in arms, so to say, Fontenelle, wrote, we shall see why such men appealed to the generation of Montesquieu. 'Who tells us about the past? Historians. Were these historians men without passions, without ignorance? Could they, even if they would, tell us what really happened?'

Here surely we may put our hand upon one of the formative movements in modern ideas, a movement in which Frenchmen played a great part and which produced in Bayle's Dictionary a great book. Whether we consult it about a place, like Naples, or a biblical character like Adam, or a Church father like Athanasius, or a party like the Pyrrhonians or an obscure figure like Rorarius or Bonfadius, we never know what we shall find. Some of the real finds are embedded in the notes, for obvious reasons, for example in the article *Hélène* we find fifty lines of text, covering eleven pages of packed notes.

Curiously enough Bayle is not a unique case in French writing. It would seem that the job he did had to be done over again, not so much for history as for science. The immense extension of scientific enquiry from 1650 onwards forced people into a new way of interpreting nature, made the old opinions out of date and a new, more cautious and reserved, view essential. So a proposal to translate Chambers' Dictionary into French gathered impetus and turned into a corporate attempt to supply a new survey of the state of knowledge. The project was committed to two first-class men, D'Alembert the mathematician, and Diderot, who had an interest in all science, an insatiable curiosity and a natural drive and energy which frequently prevented the abandonment of the whole enterprise. To read of its painful progress, of the manifold opposition it encountered, not least from Government censors, to discover that it only finally got published by eliciting the support in turn of both Jansenists and Jesuits, mortal enemies, all this reads like a novel. Perhaps it only came off thanks to two things, Diderot's enthusiastic example and the fact that it was in the mainstream of 18th-century thinking. It was in fact a glorification of reason, of the human mind that knows no limits to enquiry. As such it is one of the great books of its age. Now long superseded, it should be remembered as a pioneer in the use and dissemination of technology: the volumes of plates describing trade processes are still a joy to behold. More than this the *Encyclopédie* was a fearless book. It applied to all subjects Diderot's principle that doubt is the royal road to knowledge: 'ce qui n'a jamais été mis en question n'a jamais été prouvé'. So it glorified experiment and was sceptical about theory. Its main affirmations come out in the lucid prose of D'Alembert's preface.

To read the list of articles in the *Encyclopédie* and compare them with those in Bayle is to see how far the world of enquiry has moved in half a century. Bayle's weird unknown figures seem archaic beside such headings as *Autorité Politique, Peuple, Superstition, Traite des Nègres.* But the principles of the two works are closely similar. As Diderot said in opening his article on 'Encyclopédie': 'Ce mot signifie enchaînement de connaissance.' It seems to have been the first work in which knowledge of all kinds is put on a single level and considered as a vast interlocking structure, only possible, as he said in the same article, in a philosophic age.

It is interesting to see what these men and their epoch meant by philosophic. Not what we mean, but something nearer to experimental science. The key to their view lies in two articles, both by Diderot, *Experimental* and *Philosophie*. They took their word from Bacon, a great name in the *Encyclopédie*, as the first man who insisted on observing phenomena before drawing conclusions. Thus the word meant practical rather than theoretic, and something more. The trained observer sees single phenomena: it is for him to weave them into a system. The systems revered in the 18th century, connected with such names as Aristotle and Descartes, did not proceed from observation so much as from argument. Principles were laid down and particular cases fitted to them. This is usually known as the deductive method. Pascal, in his experiments on the vacuum, reversed the order and dared to say that in physics there are no principles save experiment itself. What he said about physics the *Encyclopédie* said on a grand scale about knowledge in general. Hence its revolutionary effect. The time had come when men had argued too much, on too narrow a front. At the cost of throwing over tradition they gave priority to observation and presented to their public a new world. For the first time in these pages one senses the possibility of new sciences, of modern chemistry and physics, even of political economy. The article on the last of these was the work of Jean-Jacques Rousseau and foreshadowed his epoch-making book *Le Contrat Social*.

This stress on experiment and observation then tells us what Diderot taught his generation to understand by *philosophie*. For them the *philosophe* was an observer who proceeded from what he called an infinite number of particular investigations. This accounts in its turn for the bias of the whole work. In the field of physical science where modern methods had so far hardly been applied, it displayed a new world of phenomena. In the traditional sciences, such as logic or jurisprudence, it was not so disturbing. In what was then thought to be the chief object of knowledge, the nature and origin of man, it seemed subversive and impious, since it set aside revelation as something which science could not control. With revelation went the authority of the Bible, which had officially been unquestioned and decisive. Only very painfully did European thinkers find their way back to some view of the true authority of Scripture.

Now we can see why the 18th century is often called the Age of Reason and why the *Encyclopédie* seems to be its most characteristic monument. As a modern scholar has said: 'the articles have to be put back in the context of the accepted outlook on the world of mid-eighteenth-century France before their full boldness is grasped.' Once this happens we see that Reason, the word and the thing, seems, in a single bound so to speak, to have come of age. It is not so much that men of genius of earlier times are refuted or surpassed. It is rather the general tone of the whole work that suggests that nothing can stand against reason, that everything should be submitted to the judgment of reason. This is not a narrow doctrine, and in 1760 it was a programme of liberation. The vast range of the *Encyclopédie* in fact did much to develop and enlarge the notion of reason. As Mr. Gendzier says: 'the philosophes fused the methods of science with what was in essence a new humanism to expand the definition of reason and also to create a new outlook on life'*.

Let us not forget that the process was not static or one of theory. It was intensely dramatic, accompanied at every stage by risk. Had it not been for the presence for so long as Controller of Printing of Malesherbes, who was both a liberal man and a friend of Diderot, the enterprise could not have avoided being stopped. Diderot indeed complained that at the last moment his printer, Le Breton, had cold feet and had let him down by excising long passages of his (Diderot's) manuscript. This we now

* *The Encyclopedia*. Editions translated and edited by S. J. Gendzier, Harper Torchbooks, 1967.

know to be true, since a copy of the final proofs has turned up in Russia, showing exactly what the printer has scored out. The praise of Bayle's *Commentaire Philosophique*, for example, as his 'best and most useful work . . . a masterpiece of reason'; this and much of the same kind had to go. And this characteristic attack on theologians:

> It is shameful that these men, whose science is full of difficulty, mystery and incomprehensibility, and who agree that without the Lord's special grace there can be no faith in what they teach, have used fire and the sword and would, if the sovereign allowed them to do so, use them again today against unfortunate men who are at most to be pitied for having been forgotten by God in the division He has made of his gifts. (Translated in Gordon and Torrey, *The Censoring of Diderot's Encyclopédie*, 1947, p. 60).

Yet the daring man who wrote this was one of the makers of our world. His work attacked many abuses, but there is another side to it. The force of the attack on religion carried the *Encyclopédie*, if we may put it so, beyond the target. They threw out the baby with the bathwater. The abiding suggestion of their volumes is not only that reason has been deprived by privilege or by tyranny of its rightful criticism. That was the case. But by comparison with the new natural sciences and the empirical method of experiment, such things as tradition, theology, dogma, even religion, were made to seem of little account. The *Encyclopédie* was too successful. It took nearly two hundred years for Europeans to recover a sense of absolute values, of the validity of religious experience and of the real nature of religion. The 19th century, which seems so sceptical an age, owed its blind spots no less than its insights to the frame of mind represented in the *Encyclopédie*.

4 Drama

IT IS NOT QUITE just to French dramatic art to consider it as being either comedy or tragedy. Some important French plays are described by neither of these words. In the 17th century the word 'comédie' meant just a play; the famous theatre is thus quite properly called: La Comédie Française. But the word *comédie* has been captured by the sense of comedy. The words used in France to denote a straight play are *spectacle* or *théâtre*, a word which in England is kept for a place and in France for a kind of art. I suggest that it is one of the French achievements to have so often and so successfully offered pleasure through a play that is neither tragic nor comic. It may be a mixture, and usually does contain elements of both, but it is chiefly a play, a good play, 'une pièce bien faite,' and its success lies in the neatness with which the three main elements of drama are welded into a single experience: author, actor and audience.

It is conveniently forgotten that the greatest box-office successes of their day were not plays by Molière or Racine but Thomas Corneille's *Timocrate* (1656) and

Lesage's *Turcaret* (1709). The first of these is built on the classical model but with a mystery about the hero; not only his intention but his actual identity is a constant source of suspense. The second is about a dishonest financier whose 'ricochet de fourberies' again are a main cause of suspense.

Those who ask what makes a play successful should study the history of a similar 19th-century success, *La Dame aux Camélias*. It was written as a novel and in desperation at not finding a publisher Dumas turned it into a play, which outdid *Hernani* and *Cyrano de Bergerac* in its record run. I think that the cause of success is here easier to pinpoint. Social criticism takes on a bite and snap and shock when brought alive on stage, as it can hardly do in the quiet pages of a novel. The shock in this case was the double standard, the prostitute introduced into formal bourgeois society. The gesture of the young man's father in refusing to raise his hat when introduced to Marguerite was said to be more gripping than any words could have been.

Perhaps we make a mistake in thinking that plays are the work of their authors. In France it is often the public that makes the play and we know that plays were written for popular actors, *Le Cid* possibly for Montdory, *L'Aiglon* for Sarah Bernhardt. At least one great classical play, *Polyeucte*, was submitted also to the criticism of a select group. In the 19th century there emerges a new figure, the *directeur de théâtre*, whose job it was to match the elements, to procure authors for plays which would be so acted that they would catch the taste of the public. Such a man was Antoine, and later Baty, and Dullin, the master of Barrault and Vilar. Such in our day have been Vilar himself, and Roger Planchon. The importance of such men suggests that drama is a living art in France. The cinema and television may have wider appeal, but the taste for life acted out on a stage seems to be a constant of French civilisation.

In a sense dramatic art is anonymous. Names appear on the hoardings but are soon forgotten. Yet the 'théâtre de boulevard,' for example, has supplied entertainment for more than a century now and those of us who are not specialists would find it hard to recall many names, either of authors or actors.

This tradition of theatrical expertise has not had to work in the void. It has proved the ideal vehicle for getting across to modern people a certain kind of play, what we might term the plays of ideas. This has been and still is one of the main attractions of the modern theatre, in London as well as in Paris. But the French excel in staging a discussion. After all, drama is an excellent medium for airing ideas. The French are full of ideas and keen on drama. Little wonder then that they have brought off a marriage of the two, which here can be no more than suggested.

Just as the effects of drama are stronger and sharper on the nerves than those of fiction, so the success of drama depends to a large measure on the luck of the first performance. Notable French plays have been denied the stage for years, or have had short opening runs. *Les Corbeaux* of Henri Becque had to wait ten years for its first playing (in 1882), was given a hostile reception and ran for only eighteen nights. Yet this fine play is a perfect example of what we are talking about. Neither comedy nor tragedy, it is a grim and fascinating re-creation of creditors descending on a widow: 'Voyez-vous quand les hommes d'affaires arrivent derrière un

mort, on peut bien dire: v'là les corbeaux.' The play still
reminds us that there are effects so stark that they need
the stage, with its paradox of devastating words quietly
spoken: 'Vous devez savoir,' says the silky lawyer to the
girl who has to be sacrificed for family solvency, 'que
l'amour n'existe pas; je ne l'ai jamais recontré pour ma
part. Il n'y a que des affaires en ce monde; le mariage en
est une comme toutes les autres.'

In a hundred years of this sort of thing the language
loosens up, becomes less stilted, more natural, but the
skill with which ideas are made alive in conflict, this is
practised in mid-20th century with constant success. The
plays of such men as Anouilh, Camus and Sartre, still
available, still performed, show how forcefully the French
renew their literary traditions. Some of us recall how
those plays were first received. It was not in a time of
boom or pride but of national humiliation, when means
were few and prospects bleak. One of my colleagues has
quoted a description of Paris in 1943, under German
occupation:

> Enfermés dans un immense camp de concentration,
> soumis au contrôle d'une armée et d'une censure
> ennemies, les Français, et singulièrement les Parisiens,
> demandèrent au théâtre l'évasion nécessaire. Ils y
> cherchèrent également une raison d'espérer dans
> cette manifestation d'une culture demeurée vivante
> en dépit de toutes les traverses. Malgré les privations,
> les alertes, les transports difficiles ou inexistants,
> pendant quatre ans on se rua au théâtre.
> (G. D. Vierge, quoted in Sartre, *Les Mouches*, ed.
> North, 1963).

To my mind Sartre is one who has used the theatre
most successfully as a pulpit, and has repeatedly shown

that it need not be any worse drama for that. How splendidly he used the old myth to imagine Orestes scorning Jupiter, that is, man judging God:

> Que m'importe Jupiter? La justice est une affaire d'hommes et je n'ai pas besoin d'un Dieu pour me l'enseigner. (op. cit. p. 106).

No scenery is needed for this kind of drama, no grand properties. Just two men facing each other. Just half a dozen women, in nun's habit, refusing to obey an archbishop. This, in Montherlant's *Port-Royal* reduced a Paris audience to tense expectancy and involvement. I am inclined to think that the last war was good for French drama. The insight of Anouilh, in his version of the Antigone story, was to see that the Germans gave new meaning to Antigone's famous 'No'.

5 Epigram

IF WE AIMED AT completeness, even a small book like this should at this point consider the French achievement in the longest and oldest form of writing, which is epic.* Since however that has no great interest we may pass to what seems its opposite, the shortest form in which words may meaningfully stand together.

The old manuals of rhetoric contrasted two extreme forms of writing. The one they called *Amplificatio*, description, ornament, eloquence in full swing, for example. The other they called the opposite, *Abbreviatio*, the art of saying much in little, of straining language to its utmost degree of compression. This kind has always attracted the French, partly because they love wit. Brevity is the soul of wit, we say, suggesting thereby that what is compressed, filed down, limited to bare essentials,

* For many reasons. The best French attempt at the epic form is medieval, in the *Chanson de Roland*. Apart from d'Aubigné's *Tragiques*, which I comment on later, and Victor Hugo's remarkable *petites épopées* known as *La Légende des Siècles*, the French do not seem to cultivate epic, except in prose fiction. Zola is an epic writer.

41

is the more startling, surprising, pregnant, teasing. These gems of compression have the power, said Nietzsche, to resist the tooth of time.

The epigram may be anonymous, a nugget of popular wisdom, like 'Man proposes, God disposes' or 'waste not want not'. It is closely allied to the proverb and the wisecrack. We still feel the charm of two words doing what most of us would need a full sentence to do: *traddutore traditore*. We still like the epigram with the sting in the tail, the single sentence that looks harmless, until the last word:

'The obscurest epoch is . . . today.' We still like (do we?) the unexplained removal to another level of what is usually thought to be a fact of experience. 'Mauvaise herbe croît toujours' means one thing to a farmer and another to us who hear it from Harpagon about his daughter. Rabelais is a master of pungent expression, as he is of many words:

> Ne souper point, dit Panurge, c'est erreur, c'est scandale en nature.

To this kind of compression Montaigne applies rare intellectual power. He too wrote much, but he liked to end the argument with a flash of wit: At times they seem frivolous, until we get the flash that lights up a civilisation:

> Nous recherchons les causes, jamais les choses. Plaisants causeurs.

Or

> Ce ne sont pas nos folies qui me font rire, ce sont nos sagesses.

Or

> Pour être plus savants, ils ne sont pas moins ineptes.

At this level, and with this skill, the epigram becomes poetic; it can reveal a world, or even two worlds side by side, the world of reputation and the world of reality, describing neither but suggesting both. To say as a judgment on society that those rated wise are fools is to say a great deal, to open a big subject, to challenge discussion. All this the epigram can achieve, in expert hands.

The pleasure of hearing something of this kind, unexplained, unqualified, sharp and bare, is a delight the French ask of their drama. It is full of challenges, single-line positions, formulae. Ronsard had shown how well the Alexandrine lends itself to this metallic and yet euphonious statement within the twelve-syllable framework:

> La matière demeure et la forme se perd.

Corneille is a master of such statements.

Part of the pleasure in seeing plays like *Horace* or *Polyeucte* performed is to wait for and to savour the single line which sums up a whole dramatic action or an emotional position. The line may even be cut:

> Que vouliez-vous qu'il fît contre trois? — Qu'il mourût.

Would it not be difficult to sum up the martyr's temperament more finely than by putting in his mouth such a line as this?

> Je consens, ou plutôt j'aspire à ma ruine.

Or the fanaticism that goes along with it:

> Je ne vous connais plus, si vous n'êtes chrétienne.

D

It was in fact the classical movement, of which Corneille was both precursor and pioneer, which perfected this form of globular and pregnant statement. No reader of Pascal can fail to enjoy his use of compressed statement, his fusion of brevity and pungency. No longer do we endure the tortuous sentences of the Renaissance style; the new effects are staccato, pungent, brief, almost to the limit of concision: 'Il n'est rien tel que les Jésuites' or 'Celui qui vous offrirait le paradis, ne vous obligerait-il pas parfaitement?' In the true Pascalian epigram we may discern a concentration of thought and a critique of language which make up a new kind of utterance:

> Le coeur a ses raisons, que la raison ne connaît point.

And

> Par l'espace l'univers me comprend . . . par la pensée je le comprends.

Is there any English writer who uses the pun in this way, not in order to amuse but to penetrate and to provoke?

Fine writing was for this fine writer incidental, not worth striving after for its own sake. Not so the late classical *moraliste* (not quite the same as moralist) La Bruyère, whose sardonic pen-pictures of the scandalous aspects of new French society have made him famous. He can render almost physical and palpable the insolence of office, the arrogance of power, the pride of rank and the morality of money. He will sketch a whole picture by physical details which suggest a moral attitude. Now and again he leaves the picture and uses the single statement, as in his parallel portraits of two men: the one is ill at ease, sits on the edge of his chair, dare not sneeze or spit or relax . . . *il est pauvre;* the other does all these

things expansively . . . *il est riche*. La Bruyère is master of
the barbed statement:

> Un dévot est celui qui, sous un roi athée, serait athée.

Or

> Dans la société c'est la raison qui plie la première.

The master of French epigram is La Rochefoucauld,
an ambitious noble, whose chances of advancement were
ruined in the civil war known as the Fronde. As con-
spirator he saw men at their worst; in the enforced
idleness of retirement, his shyness no doubt increased
by a disfiguring wound and by royal displeasure, he
delighted a select circle of ladies with his dazzling
summaries of behaviour. The society of which he had
come to know the worst supplied him with rich material:
he has piercing and often bitter comment on surface
morality, on the gap between words and deeds, profession and practice. Beneath the conventional respect
for such qualities as duty and altruism he delighted to
unveil a deep concern for one's own interest; *l'amour-
propre* was his word for this. 'On ne loue que pour
être loué' is one of his many pillule formulae.

In this remorseless exposure of the self he seems to have
stumbled upon something new in behaviour and which
since Freud has been the object of scientific enquiry, the
subconscious. 'L'esprit est toujours la dupe du coeur'
(102) is well known, but is not this as good?

> Il s'en faut bien que nous connaissions tout ce que
> nos passions nous font faire. (460)

Some of his reflexions are so new and provocative that
he has left them in a rather more loose state than the
shortest epigrams. Thus (482):

> L'esprit s'attache par paresse et par constance à
> ce qui lui est facile ou agréable. Cette habitude met
> toujours des bornes à nos connaissances, et jamais
> personne ne s'est donné la peine d'étendre et de
> conduire son esprit aussi loin qu' il pourrait aller.

Is it not a pity that the man who wrote that should be
called a cynic?

The epigram is a form of art and La Rochefoucauld's
most brilliant formulations seem due to the artist no less
than to the thinker. He obtains curious sound effects by
the repetition of a dominant consonant or vowel. For
example, the sound *i* as in n*ee*dle:

> Notre défiance justifie la tromperie d'autrui. (86)

Some of his perfect statements keep the sense and the
sting to a final word:

> C'est une grande folie de vouloir être sage tout seul.
> (231)

His great admirers, Nietzsche and Gide, have noted the
way in which he uses an almost ultimate brevity to open
up rather than to enclose a question, thus:

> La fortune et l'humeur gouvernent le monde. (435)

There are two ways of reading epigrams of this sort.
One is to pass quickly, noting little more than the neatness of word or idea. The other is to dwell on the statement, which being absolute must exclude other statements, in this case for instance that the world is governed
by a king or a council. With four operative words we
start thinking about the motives of motives, about what
lies behind a royal decision. May it not be a conjunction
of time, circumstance, and mood?

There is much more in La Rochefoucauld than the bitterness which most of us were trained to associate with him. A lady in his circle said that his *Maximes* had revealed to her a host of truths she would not have discovered in a lifetime. Voltaire, one of his admirers, cultivated and enjoyed pungency of utterance. 'Travaillons sans raisonner' suggests the nonsense of the world and the futility of explanation. *Candide* has many other cases of this compression of language. And in later writers one could follow the same manner of writing, in Vauvenargues, Chamfort, Joubert. Sainte-Beuve was inspired to add to his critical study of La Rochefoucauld fifty maximes in like manner, as a tribute. The danger of this form of writing is the cultivation of blank contradiction, on the model of 'black is white'. Paul Valéry seems to me to attempt this kind of effect, as in his epigram 'le plus profond en nous, c'est la peau'. Not so much perhaps in the acute observation: 'L'esprit clair fait comprendre ce qu'il ne comprend pas', a remark which lights up much in French education. So that one of the tests of power of epigram may be resistance to paradox. Things are not always the opposite of what they seem. There is much more than paradox, there is a world of distinction between the world of organic nature and the rough and tumble of life, in such a marvel as 'La nature fait le mérite, et la fortune le met en oeuvre'. (153)

6 Essay

ONE OF THE FRENCH TITLES to honour is to have invented the essay. There is little in classical literature that corresponds, and Montaigne preceded Bacon. The Colloquies of Erasmus and the disquisitions of Pedro di Mexia may have been the immediate models of the lifeless and brief compendia of fact and comment with which Montaigne began. A respected Bordeaux lawyer, he decided at the age of 43 to retire to his château on the hill (part of which may still be seen) and to meditate on the random thoughts which passed through his mind, in order, he says, to reduce their *étrangeté* to some sort of order. Such was the modest beginning of the two books of *Essais* published in 1580, and which, with a third book added in 1588, make up the chief prose monument of the Renaissance, apart from Shakespeare. They are the prototype of what in English we find in Bacon, Macaulay, Lamb, Aldous Huxley and Chesterton.

To compare the *Essais* with Elia is much too great a compliment to Lamb, who has little of the range and force and subtlety which make of the *Essais* one of the world's great books. It is a long way, of course, from the sketchy reflexions on 'Si le chef d'une place assiégée doit sortir pour parlementer' (I.5) to the great essays of the Third Book. But, even where he is difficult to follow, Montaigne is an enjoyable writer, informal, whimsical, quick to spring from one point to another. Many people stop here and think of the *Essais* as chatty autobiography and their author as 'the witty Frenchman', in Izaak Walton's phrase. Not so Lord Halifax (author of The Trimmer), Sainte-Beuve, Nietzsche, André Gide. Nietzsche said that the fact that an author like Montaigne had written at all increased the joy of living. If we read him with attention we shall discover, beneath the apparent disorder, a cogent and forceful mind, a thrust of thought which renews old subjects. On death, on fear, on friendship, on prayer, on books, Montaigne says surprising things. As we read we believe his preface which claimed this to be 'un livre de bonne foi' and we read his book as a sort of intellectual biography. As he charmingly said in the same preface: 'Je suis moi-même la matière de mon livre'. But this book is really no autobiography. Its real subject is man, seen through the writer no doubt, but human capacity, human limitation, man situated amid social complexity. Both subject and context are enriched by persistent reading of poetry, history and morals, and no less by close contact with administration. All this and an incomparable style, which we come to see as something which is itself the expression of a new way of looking on the world. Pascal, who was not given to praise, and who was (in the Augustinian atmosphere of Port Royal), not encouraged to praise Montaigne of all people, called the essay on conversation (III. 8) an incomparable piece of writing. Sainte-Beuve thought that Montaigne got nearer than any other man to putting Nature on paper, nature that is considered as the organic principle, not only of all created things but of man in particular. To feel the power of this writing one need only follow the argument of the essay on politics (III. i), astonishing in its fairness to Machiavelli, as in its firm disagreement. The following essay, on Repentance, performs the *tour de force* of submitting the Protestant emphasis on repentance to actual experience and formulating a notion of personality. Has it been noticed that this 'forme sienne . . . forme maîtresse', which every one of us may find within himself, is described as unique in every individual, resistant to fashion, to indoctrination and to education? We are here far from the notion of Montaigne writing about himself; we are watching the elaboration of ideas which will be taken up by Locke and by Rousseau and will thus become a part of modern educational theory.

The role of man in the world is the real subject of the *Essais*. For an expression of this in Montaigne's grand manner, the end of the essay on Vanity may serve as well as any:

(English translations are plentiful for those who desire them).

> C'était un commandement paradoxe que nous faisait anciennement ce dieu à Delphes: Regardez dans vous, reconnaissez vous; tenez vous à vous; votre esprit et votre volonté qui se consomme ailleurs, ramenez-la en soi; vous vous écoulez, vous vous répandez; appilez vous, soutenez vous; on vous trahit, on vous dissipe, on vous dérobe à vous. Vois tu pas que ce monde tient toutes ses vues contraintes au dedans, et ses yeux ouverts à se contempler soi-même?

C'est toujours vanité pour toi, dedans et dehors, mais elle est moins vanité quand elle est moins étendue. Sauf toi, o homme, disait ce dieu, chaque chose s'étudie la première, et a selon son besoin, des limites à ses occupations et désirs. Il n'en est une seule si vide et nécessiteuse que toi, qui embrasses l'univers: tu es le scrutateur sans connaissance, le magistrat sans jurisdiction, et après tout le badin de la farce. (III. 9).

This powerful suggestion of human values imperfectly known and utilised is a constant throughout the Third Book, especially strong in the final essays: *Des Boiteux*, moving from physical deformity to intellectual, *De La Physionomie* with its description *avant la lettre* of phenomenalism and of the constant confusion of appearance and reality, but most of all in the sixty pages on *Expérience*, an indictment of civilisation itself and one which Rousseau was to take up in his first *Discours*. Montaigne's case is that agencies such as education, printing, scholarship, codification (as of laws), all these have accustomed us to take life at second hand, from books or from experts or from statutes. To *experience* life at first hand, to realise that our primary activities are those of actual existence, such as eating and sleeping and daily living, this is to live in 'loyalty' as he says to the facts of the human condition. The modernity of this writing is astonishing. Who would say that the description of change which introduces (one wonders why) the essay on Repentance was written three hundred years before Proust?

It is still the fashion to read Montaigne as one will, to see in him a moralist or a romantic according to personal preference. But this is to risk misunderstanding one of the masters of French expression, one of France's 'representative men' as we might call him. Scholars owe it to the general reader to explain much more adequately than they have done why Montaigne is a classic, and what it is in him which compels attention. My own view is that in the *Essais* we find three quite distinct accomplishments which no other writer has achieved.

The first of these things I tried to express in the opening words of this section. Montaigne invented a new way of writing, a new literary genre. He gives indeed to the actual word its literal sense of a try-out, an attempt, a test. If I knew the truth, he says, 'je ne m'essayerais pas, je me résoudrais'. For him an essay was not just a few reflexions and anecdotes strung together but what he said it was: 'c'est ici l'essai de mes facultés naturelles'. We have hardly given him any credit for the fact that the essay is the only form of literary expression which admits revision, not by erasure, but by another essay. He reminds us that such is his view at the moment. Since both men and things change, 'je serai peut-être autre demain, si nouvel apprentissage me change'.

His second title to honour is that he killed scholasticism. By this I mean the time-honoured use of Aristotelian didactic methods of reasoning. Aristotle was in 1600 as in 1500 the God of the Schools. Truth was to be reached by argument, and correct argument led to the truth. This is what was shown forth in a grand way by the medieval Schoolmen, and incorporated in both school and university teaching. Long after Montaigne's time it continued to be the spirit of public instruction, but when we say Montaigne killed it we mean that he took the sting out of it by advocating another notion of truth altogether. One cannot read him without feeling that the truth is an elusive thing, not at all the servant of our logic, nor subject to laws which we have devised. All this is the subject of Montaigne's longest essay, written in defence of a book on natural theology, by Raimond Sebond. He takes up some of Sebond's points and destroys others, and turns the essay into a plea for a new scepticism, based on the little we know of the world and of ourselves. This was of course immensely stimulating to later writers like Descartes, Pascal, Bayle, Fontenelle and Voltaire. It was the first emergence of the spirit of the Enlightenment and no progress was possible until confidence in the old scholastic categories had been shaken. This Montaigne did.

But his third achievement is to my mind his greatest. He suggests the Enlightenment not only by his critique of scholasticism but by his use of what will later be known as the scientific temper and method. Montaigne himself was no scientist, but his use of data, his attitude to evidence, his sense of mysteries at present unsuspected, all these make him distrust deductive methods, arguing from the general to the particular. He prefers and actually uses the inductive method, not as Pascal's experiment will perfect it, but in a rudimentary form. He prefers particular to general statements. He thinks (see above, p. 42) that we should talk less about *causes* and more about *choses*. This very phrase could be the motto of the *Encyclopédie* discussed already in this book. More observation, more comparison, more hypothesis, less doctrinaire affirmation. He speaks as Diderot himself will speak.

To tell the story of the modern essay in French would go far beyond our scope and space here. This form of writing did not seem to catch on greatly in the classical age. Balzac wrote treatises, others wrote letters. In the 18th century Voltaire invented the philosophic tale in order to discuss ideas. It was in the 19th century that the essay form came into its own. Sainte-Beuve, Renan, Taine are all masters of the form. Their scope is more restricted than that of Montaigne. They discuss matters of scholarship, of literature, of morals. We have to wait until Anatole France to get a sprightly argument on issues of general import. But such pages as Taine's essay on Balzac, or almost any of the *Causeries du Lundi*, are as interesting as Macaulay, and more impartial, nearer to the meaning of the word *essai*. They are attempts to apply one's whole mind to the right judgment of an author or a work or a period. From such reading we emerge with a new sense of the subject, of its context in modern society or ideas, and thus with a new sense of the European tradition. Without trumpeting the fact, Sainte-Beuve was in his weekly articles slowly building up a repertoire of what he could have called 'the great tradition' of modern literature. He was far from being right in all cases. Indeed it was his misfortune to be out of tune with his most gifted contemporaries. But to read him on La Rochefoucauld, on Diderot or on De Maistre is an education. We are reading a man who himself read more widely and more searchingly than most of us ever will read. Sainte-Beuve was so good at putting opposing viewpoints that he has been called 'un homme dialogue', who saw French literature as a battleground over which the main modern ideas were fought out. He is therefore a 'key man' in any assessment of what the French have achieved.

He certainly gave new life to the French tradition of the essay. In our own day Gide and Valéry have made their own type of essay. Books like *Prétextes*, *Incidences* and the volumes of *Variété* are often in the spirit as well as the manner of Montaigne. The modern master of the form is again Sartre, whose *Situations* form a collection of essays rather different from what we have in English. To say precisely what this is would be restrictive, the one thing that a real essay is not. It may discuss any topic, it may take any view but by the end the reader should have a new view of the subject, should feel that certain traditional ways of putting things will not stand and that certain new ways are possible. English schoolboys will find it hard to believe, but our world would be the poorer without the French essay.

7 *History*

SOME OF THE FINEST French literature is history. Much of it is an attempt to recall or to interpret the past, but writers like Brantôme, Saint-Simon and Chateaubriand give us a picture of their own time: they work on what to them was the present. Much history is description. The French medieval chroniclers, Commines, some of the Romantics, the Goncourt brothers, present the past as it appeared to an onlooker. Most history is analytic, interpretative, a piecing together of fragmentary evidence. Montesquieu and Renan for instance turn their enquiries into literature, into a picture which is hardly less worth while looking at because it is wrong, and because they admit that they do not know what happened.

The modern writing of history begins with a Frenchman, Bossuet. He thought that it was possible to say not only what happened but why it happened. He had complete confidence in the Bible as giving the plan and purpose of the human story. He did this with such brilliance (his book incidentally was written for a single reader, a prince) that he provoked the first modern

historians to resist his view and to seek out other ways.
Gibbon, Voltaire, Rousseau, Montesquieu above all, all
react to Bossuet.

But it was the Enlightenment which gave them the
means to do this, and which made the writing of history
something more than description. You cannot describe
something you do not fully know nor adequately grasp.
Once admit that most of the past is lost, then you cannot
find or trace any clear pattern as Bossuet did by seeing
the history of Israel as the key to the rest. You have to
impose a pattern. Michelet, the grandest of the French
historians, thought that if you collect enough evidence
you can see an organic development working out. 'La
France a fait la France.' His Balzacian attempt is usually
reckoned a failure but it was sheer gain to literature.
After Michelet, and indeed in the latter part of Michelet's
own career, the process went astray, owing to the
materialist view of science which invaded 19th-century
thought. But even in writers as sceptical as Sainte-Beuve
and Renan this too made for fine writing.

It is in the 19th century that history really invades
literature. The works that matter are no longer only
plays and poems and novels. Alongside these the process
of investigating the past produces great books; mountains
of evidence are assembled, discussed, sifted. The human
scene is surveyed, the complexity of the human story is
made a part of the horizon of the reader. The first agents
of this process were the Romantics, under the inspiration
of Chateaubriand.

An old practitioner, Professor Gooch, thinks that few
books have had less of the historical spirit and have
stimulated that spirit more, than the *Etudes historiques* of
Chateaubriand. They are no longer read, any more than

is his novel *Les Martyrs*, or his defence of Christianity, except for the words. But it was after all the words, the style, the astonishing power of the past as he put it into words, which excited historians. Thierry could not read him without getting up from his seat and declaiming the prose. That prose fed the Romantic imagination; it inspired poems and plays. Indeed what generation could fail to be excited by the past who had the novels of Scott and the Napoleonic saga and Chateaubriand's prose on which to grow up? We can check the process from the memoirs of a sensitive spirit. Lamartine tells how at school the master put away the lesson for the day and read to them the latest arrival from Paris, a story called *Atala*. We can still read the golden phrases, the sense of mortality and temporality which made that class feel they were in a new world: 'Le temps a fait un pas et la face de la terre a été renouvelée.'

It may have been Chateaubriand who set the ball rolling but the great historian of France, from the literary point of view, is Jules Michelet. This sensitive and tormented spirit has for too long been denied his rightful place in histories of literature. That place does not depend on his style but on the fact that he wrote inspiring books, that he made history itself an inspiring thing, that he looked at history in a new way and that even when wrong (as he so often was) he wrote work of remarkable force and subtlety. He has been compared to Balzac in his range of social interest; for the Goncourt brothers he was 'un grand poète'; for Proust he was a master in the depiction of decadence.

Michelet was a passionate man, in his struggle for fame, in his sex life, in his search for documents, his speech and his writing. For over thirty years he was at the centre of

French historical investigation. His *Histoire de France*
started to appear in 1833. He completed the seventeenth
volume in 1867 and the famous Preface was added in
1869. Yet these thirty-six years were punctuated, so to
say, by a whole series of polemic and passionate works,
all of them in their way unusual, powerful, original: he
wrote on Vico (his real master, the Italian who gave him
the key to the organic principle in history), on Luther, on
the Jesuits, on birds, on women, on sorcery, all this in a
lifetime of teaching, of travel, of tireless visitation of
archives and libraries. He was famous for his hates.
Here is a characteristic outburst against England:

> Angleterre, Angleterre, vous n'avez pas combattu
> ce jour-là (i.e. at Waterloo) seule à seule; vous aviez
> le monde avec vous. Pourquoi prenez-vous pour
> vous toute la gloire? Que veut dire votre pont de
> Waterloo? Ya-t-il tant à s'enorgueillir si le reste
> mutilé de tant de batailles, si la dernière levée de la
> France, légion imberbe, sortie à peine des lycées et du
> baiser des mères, s'est brisée contre votre armée
> mercenaire, ménagée dans tous les combats et
> gardée contre nous comme le poignard de miséri-
> corde, dont le soldat aux abois assassinait son
> vainqueur? (*Histoire de France*, II. 109).

That is one facet of Michelet. His great book shows
many others which it would need ample quotation to
bring home. Let us rather listen to one of his perceptive
admirers, Edmund Wilson, commenting on the difference between Michelet and 'the ordinary historian who
knows what has happened':

> Michelet is able to put us back at upper stages of
> the stream of time, so that we grope with the people
> of the past themselves . . . are dismayed by their

E

unexpected catastrophes. . . . Michelet responds with the sensitivity of the poet to every change of tempo, movement or scope, and he develops an infinitely varied technique to register different phases. . . . I do not know of anything in literature more remarkable in its way than the skill with which Michelet leads us, as we follow generation after generation of kings, to feel the old virtue passing out of them, the lapsing of their contact with the people.

. . . The History of France stands unique, a great work of imagination and research of a kind perhaps never to occur again — the supreme effort in its time of a human being to enter into, to understand, to comprehend the development of a modern nation. There is no book that makes us feel when we have finished it that we have lived through and known with such intimacy so many generations of men. And it makes us feel something more: that we ourselves are the last chapter of the story and that the next chapter is for us to create.

(*To the Finland Station*, pp. 21, 34).

As Wilson admits, Michelet was too passionate, too uncontrolled, too visionary perhaps to realise his own grand vision. The later volumes of his history cannot keep up the promise of the first. Where his passion comes in, the facts are twisted or omitted. A remorseless analysis of his volume on Joan of Arc* leaves no doubt that he suppressed evidence in order to keep his ideal picture. He, who thought that so many factors should be brought into the writing of history, simplifies his whole central portion, the reign of Louis XIV, to an absurd degree: the King's mistresses, bastards and illnesses are

* By Gustave Rundler: *Michelet historien de Jeanne d'Arc.* 2 vols. 1925.

in the centre of his picture as if they were of 'national' importance. Yet where his prejudices were not aroused, as in the volume on the Reformation, his insights are often still valid. His writing often suggests his public image, a national figure, a white-haired prophet, turned out of his Chair at the Sorbonne for supposed incitement to sedition.

Michelet once wrote 'la méthode est tout, le sujet secondaire. Donc je pouvais prendre quinze siècles aussi bien qu'un siècle'. We must not forget that the writing of history in the 19th century was not just the affair of some gifted individuals. It was accompanied by much public discussion in which the most controversial views were thrown around. Some, like the Romantics, wanted to recover the colour of history, as they praised Walter Scott for having done. Others wanted to seek a meaning in history: 'Ici les pittoresques et là les philosophes' as one scholar has put it (P. Moreau, *L' Histoire en France au 19e siècle*, p. 97). 'Je n'aime dans l'histoire que les anecdotes' said one. Another blamed Thierry for including prices of candles and coal. Some wanted emphasis on racial differences, an aspect which Tocqueville thought most dangerous. Finally some thought real history was unattainable by research, it could only be imagined. As Balzac wrote:

> Il y a deux histoires, l'histoire officielle, menteuse, qu'on enseigne ... puis l'histoire secrète où sont les véritables causes des évènements, une histoire honteuse ... L'histoire enseignée dans les collèges est une collection de dates et de faits, excessivement douteuse d'abord, mais sans la moindre portée.
> (ibid. p. 99).

Balzac was pleading his own case and his novels certainly do give a new kind of history of the 19th century. So the argument ranged to and fro, back and forth, and the participants seem unaware that in the wings as it were was waiting a writer whose analysis of capitalistic society would be more far-reaching than any of their theories. The year 1867, which saw the completion of the *Histoire de France* saw also the publication of *Das Kapital*.

The torch of Michelet was carried on, however, in other fields of history, chiefly perhaps by one who was destined to arouse even more opposition, execration would be the word, than almost any other writer of his century, Ernest Renan. *La Vie de Jésus* appeared in 1863 and the sales, like the opposition, were enormous for the time (60,000 copies in six months). Now that the dust has settled we can see how daring was the conception of history behind this famous book: it was nothing less than the application of the canons of rational investigation to religion. And this was the first of a series, *Les Origines du Christianisme*. The title is significant, and reminds us of another title: *Les Origines de la France contemporaine*. The 19th century came a long way; thanks to its encouragement and improvement in classifying what remained of the past it could no longer be satisfied, as Voltaire had been, with looking at peak achievements of civilisation; it asked about origins. Sainte-Beuve once said: 'J'épie et note avec curiosité ce qui commence'. We shall see in a moment how he did this. (The questions here raised are discussed with great learning and insight by Marc Bloch, *Métier d'historien*, 1952).

We can see why Renan's method gave offence. He assumed, like his age, that reason was a sufficient guide to the past; he assumed that a miracle, being something not explainable by reason, could be left out of count. The confidence of these 19th-century historians in their own

interpretation of data is astonishing. It shines through all
their writing. But that does not mean that we may dismiss
their work. They are splendid reading even when they
are wrong. Taine, for example, has been most unfairly
condemned because of his theory of race, milieu and
moment. (The only historian of literature known to me
who is just to Taine is Cazamian. See some remarkable
pages in his *History of French Literature*, 1955, pp. 371–3).
If we judge Taine by his theories we should go the whole
way, and see how faithful he was to his master Michelet.
In an important preface to his book on Livy he says that
when a subject has been studied from every angle, only
then can the historian get to his proper task, that of
recalling the living past. The historian does not write to
explain, but to bring to life, to animate:

> Après avoir traversé les dissertations de la critique et
> les abstractions de la philosophie, l'historien enfin
> entre dans l'histoire. Car la vie humaine qu'il imite
> n'est pas une formule mais un drame, et les lois n'y
> agissent que par des événements. Si la copie n'est
> pas animée elle n'est ni complète ni fidèle. Que le
> passé, reconstruit par la raison, ressuscite devant
> l'imagination.

To dismiss Taine as a mere theorist is a caricature. His
history of English literature is itself literature and re-
warding to read not because of the facts (which may be
wrong) nor of the attitude (which is old-fashioned), but
because of the imaginative power that gives life to the
names of the past.

So the achievement of the French historians in the 19th
century would seem to lie in their bold use of imagination
and in their explorations into what lies behind events,

into the life of ideas. One who did this superbly denied that he had anything more than 'des parties d'historien' in his make-up. This was Sainte-Beuve. He invented a new kind of criticism but he wrote one history which is still active in its influence on readers: *Port-Royal*. The occasion of this famous book was a course of lectures given in Lausanne in 1837. An agnostic speaking before an audience largely Protestant about a Catholic monastery could not fail to come up with something interesting. And the documents (enormous reading went to the elaboration of the work) are certainly interpreted with imagination.

There is no other book like Sainte-Beuve's *Port-Royal*. He carefully did not call it a history, although it uses the methods of the historian. It is more like a portrait, of a group of men and women who seem to have had unusual effects on their age. But it is a portrait with a difference. The monastery is contrasted with its age as well as fitted into it. As we read we see that the Jansenists for Sainte-Beuve are neither friends to be praised nor enemies to be decried; they are a means of showing us what the 17th century was like; as the author put it 'une méthode pour traverser l'époque', of discovering, as he says elsewhere 'la façon de sentir de toute une famille d'esprits'. This is history of a quite new kind. It would give enjoyment to many who think of French 19th-century literature as either sloppy or sordid. It did give enjoyment to one French intellectual who read it slowly to separate himself from the realities of the last war, Montherlant. We have referred above to the play that it inspired him to write (p. 40).

The methods of Michelet seem to have inspired Sainte-Beuve to write an investigation of the past which is without the bias of Michelet. Sainte-Beuve is more like Renan in his patient accumulation of detail, and even more anxious than Renan to be impartial. In what other book may we find this habit of confronting extreme points of view, one might say clinically, 'pour mieux poser les points de départ, et maintenir les directions différentes'? It is a pity that space does not allow of a few examples of so original and powerful an approach to history.

So there is a French way of writing history as literature. Among its contemporary exponents, professors such as Seignobos, Febvre, Bloch, Mousnier, we can still feel the impetus of the great 19th-century revival. As one of them said, history is a new science.

8 *Letter*

Is IT NOT PRETENTIOUS to elevate to the dignity of a literary genre private writings between individuals, in most cases written without thought of publication? Maybe, and certainly the letter is not a literary form with rules and technique like sonnet or tragedy. The point of including it in this survey is just that French literature would be much the poorer if we could not read the letters, for example, of Flaubert, of Gide, and above all of Mme de Sévigné. Anthologies of letters have been published which show how many French writers have used this form and how much in the way of informal comment they tell us in letters about their own times. But it is one thing to read letters for information and another to read them as literature.

The survival of the Sévigné letters is a complicated story. The first thin selection appeared in 1730 and since then successive lots have been recovered and checked against copies, the largest single addition being the so-called Capmas manuscript unearthed in 1912. All older editions have been put out of date by M. Gérard Gailly's three Pléiade volumes, full of material concerning 17th-century life. Chateaubriand seems to have been irritated by this piecemeal revelation: 'Va-t-on publier encore des lettres de cette femme?' he wrote. Others have felt something of his irritation at being called upon to admire society which has long disappeared and with which our age seems to have little in common. The fact is that our reserves just do not persist if one reads with due attention. One is met by something irresistible, something not at all modern, not tender or sentimental or romantic. Put at its lowest one could call it vivacity, which in an age of classical writing is worth some attention. Things are conveyed to us with a colour, a sharpness and a sense of the particular and of restless life which we cannot for long resist. The feelings, reactions, attitudes are those of an age far away from us. The classical qualities are present, cogency, proportion, clarity, objectivity. The point is perhaps that the feelings and impressions are immediate, clear, natural. Proust was fascinated by this feature:

> . . . elle nous présente les choses dans l'ordre de nos perceptions au lieu de les expliquer d'abord par leur cause.

So he created his figure of Elstir, the painter, on the same model. Famous instances, like the letters on haymaking or on Fouquet's trial, are set for school study, but that need not prevent us enjoying them. In a day when the newspaper does not exist, a daily report on a public trial makes dramatic reading: we are told how the court is arranged, almost as a setting for the titbits of dialogue the writer is to give us. We watch the prisoner scoring off his opponents (to Mme de Sévigné's joy) to such an extent that 'M. le chancelier ne savait où se mettre.' We sense the approaching judgment and are ourselves almost persuaded that it must be an acquittal. On Friday, December 19, 1664 she reports five judges voting the death penalty, six against. Then it is seven to six, with eight still to speak, in the end nine for death, thirteen against. The suspense is conveyed as it is felt, and is the more impressive for not being written up:

> Tout le monde s'intéresse dans cette affaire. On ne parle d'autre chose, on raisonne, on tire des conséquences, on compte sur les doigts, on s'attendrit, on craint, on souhaite, on hait, on admire, on est triste, on est accablé; enfin, mon pauvre monsieur, c'est une chose extraordinaire que l'état où on est présentement . . . il faut que vous sachiez que M. Colbert est tellement enragé, qu'on attend quelque chose d'atroce et d'injuste qui nous remettra au désespoir. Sans cela, mon pauvre monsieur, nous aurions la joie de voir notre ami, quoique bien malheureux, au moins avec la vie sauve, qui est une grande affaire.

One reason why the writing is so vivid is that it is single-minded. Mme de Sévigné has no thought for any reader save one, her daughter, to whom she is entirely devoted and for whom she is concerned to give the most immediate sensation of what happens. In comparison with Mme de Grignan, the people among whom she moves do not count, especially when they are provincials: 'cette immensité de Bretons . . . me fait penser à vous'.

But the gift for vivid writing does not make a classic. Behind the impressions there is a mind, of real force, following the intellectual moves of the day, enjoying for example the satire of the *Lettres Provinciales*, faithful to

the rigorous view of life at Port-Royal, able to read
Malebranche. A 17th-century mind, content with a
hierarchy of values into which she has been born. War she
considers not with distaste but as the greatest human art.
She admires the born leader, Turenne, Condé, Louvois:

> Le voilà donc mort, ce grand ministre, cet homme
> si considérable, qui tenait une si grande place, dont le
> *moi* comme dit M. Nicole, était si étendu; qui était
> le centre de tant de choses: que d'affaires, que de
> desseins, que de projets, que de secrets, que
> d'intérêts à démêler, que de guerres commencées,
> que d'intrigues, que de beaux coups d'échecs à faire
> et à conduire. Ah, mon Dieu, donnez moi un peu de
> temps; je voudrais bien donner un échec au duc de
> Savoie, un mat au prince d'Orange: non, non, vous
> n'aurez pas un seul, un seul moment. (July 26, 1691).

Proust's Charlus was perhaps right, certainly perceptive,
in contrasting the dissolute son with the passionate
affection of the mother:

> Ce que ressentait Mme de Sévigné pour sa fille peut
> prétendre beaucoup plus justement ressembler à la
> passion que Racine a dépeinte dans Andromaque ou
> dans Phèdre que les banales relations que le jeune
> Sévigné avait avec ses maîtresses. (Pl. I. 763).

She has no feeling for the tortures applied to a sorceress.
She is honoured by every word or glance from the King.
Her description of the court performance of *Esther*
gives to perfection what was then understood by an
artistic occasion. And the references to deeper matters
are the more remarkable for coming unprepared, as the
occasion allows. 17th-century writers have almost
naturally this sense of an occasion, not least in death:

Pour M. le chancelier il est mort très assurément, mais mort en grand homme. Son bel esprit, sa prodigieuse mémoire, sa naturelle éloquence, sa haute piété, se sont rassemblés aux derniers jours de sa vie.

Now and then one comes upon the entirely unexpected, fresh, unstudied reaction to the burden of living:

Rien n'est si fou que de mettre son salut dans l'incertitude; mais rien n'est si naturel, et la sotte vie que je mène est la chose du monde la plus aisée à comprendre. Je m'abîme dans ces pensées, et je trouve la mort si terrible que je hais plus la vie parce qu'elle m'y mène que par les épines qui s'y rencontrent. Vous me direz que je veux vivre éternellement. Point du tout; mais si on m'avait demandé mon avis j'aurais bien aimé à mourir entre les bras de ma nourrice: cela m'aurait ôté bien des ennuis et m'aurait donné le ciel bien sûrement et bien aisément; mais parlons d'autre chose.

(Pl. I. 497).

She has this in common with other 17th-century writers, that individualism is held of little account and only in the private letter and under provocation does one get anything like a confession. The letters of Saint Vincent de Paul for instance show the burdens he bore rather than any personal reaction to them. Those of Gui Patin tell us less about the writer than about the medical profession in Molière's day. Such 'real' letters contrast sharply with the rhetorical letter intended for public reading, such as gained a great reputation for Guez de Balzac.

But to find another sequence of letters as brilliant as those of Mme de Sévigné we must wait for Fénelon and still more for Voltaire. The amazing energy of Voltaire comes out constantly in his letters. 'This frail dynamo', as he has been called, writes 'as he lived' in perpetual animation, restless, keen, enquiring into a hundred matters at the same time. His great admirer, Flaubert, was also a most voluminous letter writer. After a day spent in literary labour he will write a letter of several close pages, and not many fail to touch upon important issues of art and criticism. They give us the pleasure of reading the comments of a fine and delicate mind, in a modern world this time. Listen to him on the literary doctrine he is supposed to have introduced and perfected, realism:

> Quant à laisser voir mon opinion personnelle sur les gens que je mets en scène: non, non, mille fois non. Je ne m'en reconnais pas le droit. Si le lecteur ne tire pas d'un livre la moralité qui doit s'y trouver, c'est que le lecteur est un imbécile ou que le livre est faux au point de vue de l'exactitude. Car du moment qu'une chose est vraie, elle est bonne. Les livres obscènes ne sont même immoraux que parce qu'ils manquent de vérité. Ça ne se passe pas 'comme ça' dans la vie.
>
> Et notez que j'exècre ce qu'on est convenu d'appeler le réalisme, bien qu'on m'en fasse un des pontifes; arrangez tout cela. (1876).

English readers will find passages that explain much of what we find in French books:

> Je viens de lire *Pickwick* de Dickens. Connaissez-vous cela? Il y a des parties superbes; mais quelle composition défectueuse. Tous les écrivains anglais en sont là. Scott excepté, ils manquent de plan. Cela est insupportable pour nous autres Latins. (1872).

It takes a great writer to use such informality and yet to keep his matter so intelligent and cogent. Perhaps this section should not be on the Letter so much as on the French modes of criticism, which we have already sampled in the historical field. At any rate the Letter as a means of discussion is taken further in our own century, by André Gide, Valéry, Claudel, Rivière. It thus becomes a typical and modern form of French literary expression.

9 Novel

HE WOULD BE A BOLD MAN who attempted today what George Saintsbury did seventy years ago, a history of the French novel. In the far off days of Queen Victoria French novels were apparently read as a risky form of literature, not as art but as sensation. Until recently they had a freedom (particularly of sexual description) which English novels lacked. It is important not to get the sensational and the really artistic elements mixed up. The French are after all responsible for some of the great novels of the world; their experiments with the exciting and dangerous possibilities of fiction are worth serious study. Henry James, not only a master artist but a student of his art, wrote some of his best essays on the French novelists and considered the French as masters in the art of fiction.

The novel is, one might say, the giant among literary genres. It has in output dwarfed every other; it has taken into itself the qualities of epic, drama and satire. It seems to have no rules; a novel can apparently be anything and about anything, that is not in verse. It is difficult for some people to think of novels as planned at all. They speak as if novels were just stories, which either happened as they are told or came to the writer as he wrote. Such people need, and in universities I hope they get, a course of study in Flaubert's letters. For others, the only problem about novels is realism: could this happen so? Could there be such people? Are they 'real'?

Yet we should be very unfair to the greater French novelists if we were to forget that the novel has an aesthetic. It is a structure, in and of words. It is planned and formed by an artist. Things in novels do not just happen; they are made to happen; they are arranged in a meaningful sequence; they lead to a climax. How many people have begun to write a novel and found that their third chapter was less interesting than the first two? The charm of the novel may be precisely that it is not real, not like life. In the story, James Bond cannot lose, Robinson Crusoe will survive.

The chapters of a novel, said Virginia Woolf, are an attempt to construct something as controlled as a building. This point is often forgotten. Watch what E. M. Forster calls 'the difference between people in life and people in books'. The novelist juggles with psychology, with topography, most of all he juggles with time, in order to get the effect he wants. Sometimes that effect is one of sensation: many thrillers have no more than this. True art demands other things, such as form, pattern, unity. How do the greater French novels come off if we apply these standards? I think we may assume that this kind of art, like others, has been slowly perfected by long practice. The Middle Ages had stories, but not I think novels in our sense. The Renaissance produced what I would call the first French novel. It is called *Gargantua and Pantagruel.* Rabelais is a great writer, but a novelist almost by accident. He was experimenting with a parody of the prose romance in which giants did marvellous things. In many ways his book is not a proper novel. Its plot is thin; the episodes are haphazard; there is little connexion between the chapters. The matter of these chapters delights us for quite other reasons than say the art of a novel by Jane Austen. It is a picture of French life, at times quite close to the real thing. It is also a work of fantasy, in which anything may happen. This makes unity hard to attain but it allows a great writer to display astonishing variety of style. Burlesque, satire, mockery of contemporary ideas, a wonderful voyage, a grand sense of comedy, all these are in Rabelais. He gets little credit for having put side by side in one story an ideal man, giant, Renaissance prince and intellectual rolled into one, and his servant, a mean rat of a man, inventive, immoral, entertaining; Panurge is one of the great characters of literature.

In Rabelais as in Cervantes we see some of the new things that the novel can do; notably it can supply a story more interesting than the medieval romance, and more interesting to different kinds of people. The French wrote novels of all kinds, partly because of Rabelais; stories that were fantastic, down to earth, improving, risky, containing moral precepts or thinly disguised models of aristocratic behaviour. Saintsbury found this last type both dull and interminable. That was because he did not know the real figures behind the books, and because modern novels had made him think that stories should not drag. But the point of the 17th-century novel was to drag, like an endless serial, to supply more and more material for polite discussion. Thus grew up the notion

F

that novels were for women to read; men had no time. Some of the great French novels have been planned to resist this conception of the novel as a gentle interminable flow of narration intended for people with time on their hands.

The masterpiece of the French novel in the 17th century seems built on the opposite principle. *La Princesse de Clèves* is a short book, with so little incident that the author, Mme de La Fayette, had to introduce extra stories, as Dickens and Balzac and Cervantes were also to do. But it is the more effective for its brevity; the single theme comes out all the more strongly, and that theme is simple and tragic. It is the invasion of a relatively happy marriage by ungovernable affection. The formality in behaviour, the delicacy of the main character, these only intensify the tragedy. For as an honourable woman she thinks it right to confess to her (also honourable) husband that she loves someone else. By mischance, or by the chance that makes a novel, that someone is almost present, hidden outside the window. He cannot help spreading what he hears, so both husband and wife feel that the other has betrayed a private conversation and the net result of the resolve to be honest is that the situation is much worse. This is not to us very exciting, our palate is sated, but this indictment of marriage, for the story amounts to hardly less than that, is still impressive because the subject is so firmly seized and economically told.

In the 18th century we can see the novel developing into a dominant means of literary expression. All kinds of novels were written but only five or six have kept enough life in them to interest the non-specialist. Of these the adventures of *Gil Blas* by René Lesage is perhaps the best story, Prévost's *Manon Lescaut* the most finished and artistic, Voltaire's *Candide* the most hard-hitting as a novel of ideas. Voltaire's invention, as an aid to his propaganda campaign to make people think for themselves and to resist authority of church and dogma, was to write a philosophic tale, offering almost a kaleidoscope of the world's ills, but told with such humour and vitality that the effect is not depressing. Voltaire inherited Molière's gift of the immortal phrase. His innocent hero is made (against all likelihood) to watch the execution of Admiral Byng; he persists in asking why this should be and finally gets this answer:

> . . . en ce pays il est bon de tuer de temps en temps un amiral pour encourager les autres.

Voltaire excels in putting side by side tedious arguments about harmony and calamities and crimes. The book ends as Candide, tired of his mentor proving all has been for the best in the best of all possible worlds, is left with only this to say:

> Cela est bien dit, répondit Candide, mais il faut cultiver notre jardin.

In some ways the most famous novel of the 18th century continues the theme of *La Princesse de Clèves*. Rousseau shows in *Julie, ou la nouvelle Héloïse* natural love crossed by parental command. The first part, showing the idyll of two young people in love amid the most magnificent scenery, became a source book for romantic poets and was wildly popular. The second part, showing the necessity of marrying a partner chosen by the parents, was more to the taste of the moralists. The whole book, as one scholar has shown, described the opposite of contemporary mores and made bold suggestions as to restoring the reputation of marriage. Rousseau exposed as dangerous the segregation of the sexes before marriage; no less trenchantly did he expose the code of laxity after marriage. It may have been the Calvinist in him which advocated free choice of marriage partner and strict fidelity once marriage had been entered on.

Less moral, less propagandist but a finer work of art was *Les Liaisons Dangereuses*, by Laclos, long condemned as an immoral book but now being studied as a masterpiece. The remorseless delineation in a series of interlocking letters of self-seeking allied to intelligence makes an impressive picture of what Pascal would have called 'la misère humaine'. The control is perfect and would show if there were need that by 1787 the French had discovered ways of making the novel do things which the Renaissance would have thought impossible.

The Romantic writers used the new instrument perfected by the novelists of the 18th century as a means of self-expression. The short tales of Chateaubriand, *Atala* and *René*, and still more that of Benjamin Constant, *Adolphe*, are perfect recreations of a state of mind. Romantic melancholy, desire for escape, emotional dissatisfaction, this complex mood finds in such fictional confessions a perfect, beautiful expression. The example of Walter Scott was to show yet another way forward for the novel in the attempt to recover the colourful illusion of the past. Alexandre Dumas is not reckoned a great artist yet he made French history accessible and entrancing to generations of readers.

But the curious and unexplained thing about French literature in the early 19th century is that there were major novelists who achieved some sort of synthesis of these conflicting trends. Stendhal for example gave to his wonderful book *Le Rouge et le Noir* this subtitle: *Chronique de 1830*. We find that we are reading not just the adventures of a gifted young peasant who tried the Army and the Church and found no settled career, but the unrest following the July Revolution, in which class struggle seemed to be the one social law, and in which a low man was prevented from making his way into other strata of society. We feel that we are getting near Marx, and still more so in the novels of Balzac.

When Balzac started writing in the 1820s the novel seemed to have reached an impasse. The sensational story, the realistic picture of low or ordinary life, personal confession, all these had been tried and seemed exhausted, or without promise for future development. Readers had tired of all these and it was not easy to find new ways of writing stories. Were they to be improving, or shocking, or personal? Balzac was uniquely equipped to solve this dilemma, and to put the novel on a new footing. His lack of education and his personal vanity have prevented many readers from recognising that here was a genius of rare gifts. Baudelaire and Henry James and Dostoievski were certain of this, but many teachers, especially in England and America, are not yet convinced of it. More than any other novelist Balzac seems able to invent the real. He cannot have seen all that he describes, yet his pictures of places and people and ways of life are so convincing that his work is a social history of France in his time. Yet he had to a fantastic degree the inventive faculty. He seemed to be tireless in thinking out new stories. Over eighty he actually wrote out on paper, but he died leaving some forty more sketched or planned.

Has there ever been such a human machine, and one so capable of supplying what the early 19th-century novel most needed, a fusion of sensation and realism? In its later stages what he had created seemed to be something more than novels, so (whether with Dante in mind or not) he gave it a single title, suggesting that all stories were fragments of the one great story of humanity, *La Comédie Humaine*.

It is a pity that more people have not in our day learned how to read Balzac. Taken in small doses he is not more impressive than Dickens and (to us at least) less likeable (but see Flaubert's letter in Chapter 8). It is when one gets away from the few best known ones to discover novel after novel that one is impressed by the range of interest, the number of situations, the illusion of living people in quantity. And, with all this, unforgettable confrontations (incidentally very French and at times classical), scenes that remain in the mind because they are locally situated, in actual Paris or in the provinces, carefully prepared and acutely seen. In going over this point I found myself making a list of these that had so impressed me: Rastignac challenging Paris, Chabert cheated of his wife, Grandet's war against his daughter, Claes sacrificing family to chemistry, Philippe Bridau outwitting both his artist brother and family plotters in Issoudun, beating the clique of Issoudun at their own game, peasants victorious over their landlord, Pons cheated of his pictures, Birotteau's fight for solvency, his brother's fear of a landlady, the blind flute-player's dream of Venice. . . . One could go on for much longer, and still risk omitting someone's favourite. If this book were longer it might be worth while explaining how the miracle was accomplished. That would not be easy but I think it would support the judgment of Henry James that Balzac stands apart, as the greatest of French novelists.

Someone has remarked how lucky French novelists are in having the French to write about. Since 1850 three major artists, and many excellent craftsmen, have taken the novel into ways unknown to Balzac. The first of these is Gustave Flaubert, of whose letters we have already spoken but whose two great novels, *Madame Bovary* and *L'Education Sentimentale*, would need a book to themselves. A more careful artist than Balzac, chiselled, impersonal, fearful of over-writing or of showing his own opinion, a master of artistic realism, in whom the description is so careful and lifelike that one does not know whether a country fair or a cab-ride in Rouen is a picture or a symbol. Why should we decide? The point is that the novel in Flaubert's hands has mastered new techniques, is becoming able to reflect the delicate and complex issues of modern life. Emma is like many village girls, as Homais is a satire of many provincial shop-keepers, and yet unforgettable, something brought into existence by no other artist. Flaubert thought that every sentence, indeed every word, mattered in the work of art. At the end of his life he tried his hand at three tales ('pour voir si je puis encore faire une phrase') which some of us find among the most perfect works of French art. A student who seeks by a single example to see what a great writer can achieve should study Flaubert's retelling of the death of John the Baptist, not, as in the Gospel, with any conviction as to whether he was in the right, but showing him in prison, the plaything of intrigue and jealousy at an Eastern court, everyone else afraid or ashamed or plotting or cautious, the one man whose life

is in most danger completely careless of it, a stern
fanatic, counterpart to all the rest.

Emile Zola's work is again in great contrast to that of
both his great predecessors. No wonder, for he was
unbalanced in personal matters, and over-impressed with
new scientific discussions of heredity that convinced him
he could make the novel a case study of how the people
live. At the same time he was a writer with gifts of epic
vision. His marvellous descriptions of the French defeat
in 1871, of country life on its sordid side, of ginshops,
stores, miners, all these make his series of novels about
the Rougon-Macquart family into a single great, if at
times unpleasant, epic achievement. To gauge his power
one could compare two stories on much the same theme,
Zola's *Thérèse Raquin* and Dreiser's *American Tragedy*.

Anyone who knew Marcel Proust just before the
First World War would not have thought him capable of
writing anything as fine as the three artists we have just
considered. But then that 'anyone' could not have known
that for years Proust had been fighting his asthma and
using social outings as a cloak for a novel in an entirely
new manner. His abandoned first attempt is now available
as *Jean Santeuil* and one marvels that an apparent invalid
could have cast aside so long a work and have committed himself to a rewriting on a Balzacian scale. The six
huge novels which make up *A la Recherche du Temps
Perdu* present an imaginative picture of French society,
and alongside that a new view of human social relations.
The novelty seems to rest on the simple discovery that
you can never really know anybody. We are all different
people, even to ourselves. Every face, as he says in one
place, has a hundred different masks. People in Proust
are always other people, new people, as the final words

of his book say, 'giants immersed in Time', living on what they have forgotten, in touch with what a chance movement may reveal.

For a second (and if one thinks of Saint-Simon a third) time the French have made a *Comédie humaine*. Proust is already a classic and the novelists of our own century have gone different ways. The French have indeed invented a new novel, written around objects, scrutinising details, using consciousness to make something quite different from what most people want from a story. For the moment experiment has left the fictional to deal with impressions and analyses. We must remember that any new school or manner is only one experiment among many, and that the French, indeed the European, practice of fiction is now so abundant that there are novels for all tastes, recovering the past (the historical novel has been widely practised in this century), inventing new worlds of fantasy, close at hand in the regions of France, faraway in space, a context of great modern problems and a means of controversy, all these forms has the novel taken. Wisdom lies for most of us perhaps in looking afresh at the great achievements of the past and picking from the present output what suits our taste. With the single word of warning that if we are to be just to this splendid form of French art we must not read for the matter, as one chooses a tale in a public library, we must try to envisage a work of art. Reading a novel, said Virginia Woolf, is itself a difficult and complex art.

10 *Nouvelle*

WE MEET A DOUBLE TEMPTATION at this point and I hope nobody will be offended that I break the alphabetic order by considering the short story just after the novel, from which I suppose it derives. Why not call it *Short Story* and deal with it later? The fact is that we need a new word in English, a word that the French, the Germans and the Italians use to great effect. By using their word in our language I wish to stress that the short story as an art form is not just not as long as most novels. The difference in fact between great short stories and novels is not, as the words suggest, one of length, but of nature. Let me dwell for a moment on this point.

I once asked a class to draw up in parallel columns the differences of treatment which are imposed on the writer of a *nouvelle* as distinct from a novelist. We were surprised at the list that emerged. Starting from the obvious fact that the novelist has all the time and space he needs for his narration and that the writer of a nouvelle must be brief, we found that he must be several other things as well. He must prefer summary to detail, choice to quantity. He must use speed rather than time. He has no time for explanation, no time for preparation. Instead therefore he gives us unexplained the mysterious, the unprepared, the blunt fact, the sensation. He will have to prefer showing to telling, atmosphere to people, symbols to things, what is vivid to what is convincing, what strikes us quickly and powerfully rather than what we come to feel to be true. These are large differences. If we put them sharply by saying that the nouvelle works with power and the novel with truth, we might feel that was going too far. But the statement would be valid for Edgar Allen Poe and partly so for Kipling.

When we see that these two forms of art need two quite different techniques then we can remove from our new category stories that merely happen not to last very long. Voltaire's *Contes* for instance are a brilliant invention, employing surprise and shock, but they are not stories 'for the story'; they are means of argument. Certain Romantic short stories like *René* or *Adolphe* are personal confessions. If we judge them according to the criteria we have been listing, we do not get at their real merit and we obscure the fact that the French have achieved great things in the handling of brief fiction. As with their epigrams the brevity is not an accident, it is a means of increasing power, of screwing up the effect.

In my own experience Balzac is here again the master. I cannot imagine a serious student reading *Le Colonel Chabert* without asking himself why he is so fascinated and held by a story which from any of us he would dismiss as hopelessly unlikely. This is because Balzac has used subtle means to overcome our disbelief, just at the points where it would have been decisive. He does not say that his hero was left for dead on the battlefield of Eylau and brought up by Polish peasants. He gives us a close up of the hero arriving, down at heel and mocked by the clerks, at his lawyer's Paris office. Balzac admits that this odd man has a very odd story to tell, so odd that the lawyer, with no leisure in a busy day, makes an appointment with him for one in the morning. There, between man and man, in the silence of the deserted office, the whole story is told. We are given no chance to reflect and sit back and protest, for the story is more than unlikely: it is challenging, symbolical almost, far-reaching. The lawyer is convinced (note this) that the man before him is actually the Colonel who was taken for dead after the battle and whose wife has re-married. His identity is clear, he has a right to his fortune. Can he recover it in law? All means are tried. The first title of the story was *La Transaction*, the compromise. The wife defeats this, the law admits the impasse, the colonel retires to an almshouse. The injustice is clear, but equally so is the nature of society moving on its ponderous way and unable to undo what has been entered into by contract, unable to put the clock back, even for the best of reasons. I have yet to find a reader who gives this story a fair trial and does not in the end admire what he reads. Here is realism applied to the immediate impression, even against all likelihood. And is it all so unlikely? This is perhaps Balzac's strongest card: in the France left by Napoleon anything may happen. Or as he put it later in the preface to the *Comédie Humaine*: 'le hasard est le grand romancier, on n'a qu'à l'étudier.'

Paul Bourget was impressed with Balzac's power of making the issue raised by his story loom so large that we forget to question doubtful points. Zola admired *Le Chef d'oeuvre Inconnu* (and incidentally wrote his story

about the artist, *L'Oeuvre*, with it in mind) and here again
we may study the various devices whereby we are given
the illusion of reality that is not only fixed in time but
suggestive of something outside time, no less than the
nature of art. The story concerns the painter Frenhofer
who consents to show his young protégé Poussin the
picture on which he has spent his whole life. When
unveiled there is nothing to be seen on the canvas; bit by
bit the whole thing has been painted over, and painted
out, except a marvellous foot in a corner which has
escaped attention.

Technically perhaps the story called *La Grande Bretèche*
is an even finer achievement than these two. The crimes
which took place in the house are slowly extracted, but the
entry to the house itself is as slow and difficult as our
approach to the events. It is fenced off, overgrown, falling
into decay, the home of vermin, a ruin. 'Une invisible
main a partout écrit le mot *Mystère*'. Is it only the house
that is meant, or the story?

Beside such mastery the stories of Alfred de Vigny
about the military life look amateur, but I wonder
whether they are not among his most successful writings.
Three stories, all historical, interspersed with comment,
which is autobiographical at times, but deepened by
Vigny's sense of the historic moment, the boy behind the
curtain at the interview between the aged Pope and the
new age, in the person of General Bonaparte.

Flaubert's three Tales, written at the end of his life,
seem to me to use these possibilities of the nouvelle, not
so impressively as Balzac perhaps but with a beautiful
fusion of effects and all three constructed on much the
same pattern. With extreme realism we are shown a
suggestion of something quite unrealistic, more in the

domain of the mind than of the external world. Flaubert delights to imagine polarities, apparent incompatibles. We have seen how his John the Baptist is impressive as a fanatic surrounded by sycophants. In *Un Coeur Simple* the old servant is the ne plus ultra of devotion and fidelity, and at the same time of appalling stupidity, happily imagining the Holy Spirit in the form of her favourite parrot. The most remarkable of the three stories claims to retell a legend in a church window, the wonderful life of Saint Julian, who was both sinner and saint. We are shown the utmost sadism and (surely as counterweight) the ultimate in renunciation. Julian is a great killer, of animals and even of his own parents. Yet the final description of the rescued leper inviting him to lie and warm him with his own body is nearly unbearable to read.

Flaubert was the first to recognise Maupassant's *Boule de Suif* as a masterpiece. Despite the unpleasant subject this must be one of the finest of French nouvelles. Its satire of middle class people in a bus, scorning the prostitute until they discover that they may share her lunch, then actually urging her to yield to the German officer as a condition of their freedom, and finally as the bus returns despising her once more . . . all this, told with the utmost economy, achieves a powerful effect. Maupassant was able to attain such effects time and again. *The Piece of String*, *The Necklace*, *The Vendetta*, *At Sea*, *The Olive Grove*, all these are perfect achievements and not all are sordid or even pessimistic. In view of Maupassant's bad reputation one should read the charming sketch called *Minuet*, in which an old man met by chance in the park is asked what a minuet was, and produces a companion and a demonstration.

Since the end of the 19th century the nouvelle has been brilliantly applied to various uses. Gide has used it for ironic argument, Camus for that astonishing recreation of a teenager which is also a strong indictment of modern society, called *L'Etranger*, Sartre in his collection *Le Mur* for vivid political and social criticism. This is perhaps the real point to make: the French have used this form with great variety. Not all 19th-century stories are like those quoted above. Villiers and Supervielle write very different nouvelles from Flaubert and Maupassant. But all these writers put to brilliant use the conditions of the nouvelle, the concentration made possible by economy of narration and what we may perhaps call inscrutability of subject; absence of development increases surprise. The emotion of shock is often the source of pleasure.

11 Poem

IF THIS WERE A GUIDE to French literature, this section might well be the most important of all. The French skill in the handling of words has been most daring and most exciting in their poetry. This is not the usual view. Voltaire and Mme de Staël are each quoted as having said that French literature was chiefly a prose literature. This may have been because the great experiments of the French in poetry were to come after their time, although fashions in taste prevented them from enjoying Villon and Ronsard, and even La Fontaine as a poet. To present 'French poetry in a nutshell', as a friend of mine remarked, introducing a pleasant anthology (*Des Vers de France*, selected by Laurence Bisson. Penguin, 1942), is a sure way to destroy its appeal. Not only so, but in a day of expert selections and critical analyses anyone who cares can provide himself with both the poetry and the means of approaching it. In a sense therefore this is the least important section of the present book, since its matter can be easily had elsewhere and in more satisfying detail.

What I would rather do here is to suggest a few key-points and comment on some of the greater names so that the general picture be not out of balance. To embrace as it were in a single glance the whole sweep of French poetic achievement is an inspiring sight, which should not be denied to the beginner. For in cultivating the poem, as the novel, the French have, over quite a long period of nearly five hundred years, shown remarkable powers of renewal. We need not go by centuries, although they have become the most handy divisions of modern culture, but time and again there have come along poets who have given to old forms a new content, who have made poems delightful in their novelty and in their appeal to contemporary taste. There is nothing marvellous about this but it would be a pity to forget it. And when it occurs repeatedly we are entitled to say that a nation shows not only poetic powers but powers of poetic renewal. This kind of renewal was, I suggest, accomplished by Ronsard during the Renaissance, by La Fontaine in the classical period, by Lamartine and Hugo and others in the Romantic period, by Baudelaire in mid-19th century, by Mallarmé in an age of scientific realism and by Valéry in our own century. To speak of contemporary poets is not for anyone who has passed middle age to do. I am of those who think that contemporary literature should not be taught; it should be enjoyed by those for whom it is written, the young. When it has settled down and passed into some perspective, then is the time for academics to write its 'history'.

One way to appreciate Ronsard and his fellow poets is to realise how harsh an age the Renaissance was. For many, life was little more than drudgery, ignorance of medicine made death present and likely; the life span of

G

many was short. Living could be enjoyed only by the rich and leisured, and for one of them there were scores of people living a low-level existence, little more than subsistence. It is quite a shock to realise that *Gargantua*, with its joy in food and drink, was written for readers who were hungry. As if life were not hazardous enough, war and civil war took their toll. Both meant plunder and savagery that have now disappeared from Europe. It was in such a time that Ronsard proposed a new kind of poetry. He disregarded, perhaps unfairly but we can now see why, the pleasant rhymes of Clément Marot, and advocated classical study, that is study of the poets of Greece and Rome, as the way to a new kind of enjoyment in words. He studied the rhymes and vocabulary and detail of such poets as Pindar and Horace and Catullus, and decided that there can be a poetic language as well as a language for the prose uses of every day. This new language was what he instructed his friend Du Bellay to 'sell' in a famous manifesto *De la Défence et Illustration de la Langue Française* (1549). This must have been the case, for to say with the pages of Rabelais before them that the French tongue was 'pauvre et nue' was absurd. The French sense of a poetic language was indeed, when Ronsard started, almost non-existent. By new forms of poem, odes, sonnets, *hymnes*, discours, elegies, and even by epic he taught his generation to feel pleasure in rhythmical, suggestive, words. This was to open the gate into a new and strange world, a world of beauty, when most people found in actual living too little beauty.

I think that a study of Ronsard's rhymes and poetic vocabulary will bear out what I say. In his first preface he took care to dissociate himself from contemporary poetry, saying he could have nothing to do with 'so monstrous an error'. Those of us who find pleasure in reading Marot feel this to be unfair, but perhaps no other course was open to Ronsard. Marot was a poet of the Wordsworth type, who saw in common things and ordinary words the material of a poem. At times he brings it off splendidly. But he thought of poetry as a pastime; for Ronsard it was a priestlike vocation. 'Ronsard,' said one scholar, 'reverses the Wordsworthian programme', that is, he stresses the otherness of the poetic world, accessible only through words used in a new way, not soiled by daily use. How close this is to the views of Mallarmé. I would say that the Pléiade achieved a revolution in taste of the same kind as the Symbolists achieved. Of all this, an example as good as any is supplied by Ronsard's best known poem, the ode 'Mignonne, allons voir', of which an expert has written this:

> 'pas une image, presque pas un mot dont on ne puisse se rendre compte par les lectures de Ronsard, mais rien de trop, rien de moins, une tournure originale, un organisme nouveau, . . . merveille de logique et d'esprit . . . en trois mouvements pleins de grâce et d'harmonie'.
>
> (P. Laumonier, *Ronsard poète lyrique*, p. 589).

In a sense the greater French poets seem to have all been very much in Ronsard's position of having to create a new kind of poem, of finding poetry in an impasse, where the convention of their day did not allow them to say what they had it in them to say. La Fontaine was faced with a choice (experts have shown this) between the frivolity of Précieux verse and the heaviness of rhymed moral precept. His contemporaries cultivated the epic, in which marvellous adventures were recounted at length, but which of their efforts has survived? La Fontaine had to find a way forward for poetry, and did so with the classical use of the Fable. To this he brought a mind matured by reading and reflexion, a sense of the naïve, a taste and a daring which should make the study of his poems a delight, instead of the dull process which it often is. The very notion of men as animals, men who are not men, animals who argue, puts us in a world where all is indeterminate and attractive by its novelty; only an artist of great imaginative power could accomplish this. It leaves him free to render the sights and sounds of his own day with acute realism. For example the stage coach:

> Dans un chemin montant, sablonneux, malaisé,
> Et de tous les côtés au soleil exposé
> Six forts chevaux tiraient un coche.
> Femmes, moine, vieillards, tout était descendu . . .

Yet a banality is changed into a Virgilian resonance by two Alexandrines:

> Celui de qui la tête au ciel était voisine
> Et dont les pieds touchaient à l'empire des morts

The poet is free to describe in his own, very own, way the multiple pleasures of poetry:

> J'aime le jeu, l'amour, les livres, la musique.
> La ville et la campagne, enfin tout; il n'est rien
> Qui ne me soit souverain bien,
> Jusqu'au sombre plaisir d'un coeur mélancolique . . .

But this is not the romantic expansion for which it may be taken; it is part of a hymn to pleasure, that pleasure

which he sought as the charm and bloom of the slightest
tale. La Fontaine was a poet for whom pleasure without
what he called instruction was no pleasure. We should
study what he meant here. Not, I suggest, a 'moral' in any
usual sense, but a certain poise and perspective given to
the particular subject by a glimpse into the nature of
things. The old tale of Circe and Ulysses is not so much
retold as recalled, by one who fears that men might be
reluctant to change back to beasts. 'The man and the
snake' calls up a vision of dominance which suggests the
terrifying, but does no more than suggest. *Le Paysan du
Danube* dares to address the Roman senate, but no state
can stand such independence for long. The dying lion is
so vaguely described that we catch the very breath of
passing greatness. The new Royal Society of London is
mocked for summoning the King to see mountains on the
moon, which turn out to be a mouse in the lenses of their
telescope. Fantasy of this range is rare; it calls for great
gifts of phrase and for poetic vision. It was strong
enough in Jean de La Fontaine to enable him to present
within tales and fables something which he called *Volupté*
but which we might translate not too badly by poetic
pleasure; the only way, in the France of 1670, which any
Frenchman found of rediscovering poetry as Wordsworth
described it, 'the breath and finer spirit of all knowledge'.

Such also was the task and achievement of Lamartine,
who in 1820, after a prose poet like Chateaubriand had
taken him part of the way, to an overintellectualised
society restored the music of words, the experience of
solitude, the magic of melancholy. All these changes were
known to La Fontaine, no doubt, but all lacked expression
in new, unsoiled terms. What would one not give, in a
troubled and confused age, when the noise of urban

civilisation invades everything, to hear for the first time such lines as these:

> Mon coeur est en repos, mon âme est en silence;
> Le bruit lointain du monde expire en arrivant,
> Comme un son éloigné qu'affaiblit la distance,
> A l'oreille incertaine apporté par le vent.
>
> (Le Vallon)

Literary science has not yet advanced to the point of explaining how and why it was that alongside Lamartine there seemed to spring forth a whole school of poets, Vigny, Musset, Victor Hugo—one of the most amazing poetic temperaments literature can show, a man who could see in common things as in fantastic visions a glimpse of the eternal beauty. Like many of my generation I was badly brought up to grasp such poetry as that of Hugo. I was directed to *what* he said and only later found that this did not much matter. When read aloud the words suggested something much more poetic than what they meant logically.

The romantic renewal of poetry is somewhat dwarfed in our eyes by the emergence in the 1860s of protests even more powerful against the material world. We can see now that Gérard de Nerval and Baudelaire were preparing what seems to have been the greatest of all revolutions in the French cultivation of poetry, a movement which is known as Symbolism. The sonnets of Nerval, it has been said, 'forgotten by the world for nearly fifty years, were all the while bringing new aesthetics into French poetry . . . for the first time words were used as the ingredients of an evocation, as themselves not merely colour and sound, but symbol'. (Arthur Symons, *The Symbolist Movement in Literature*, pp. 37, 34).

On Baudelaire, one of the most important figures in any account of French literature, I prefer to let an expert speak:

> If a single volume had to be chosen through which to approach French poetry, the *Fleurs du Mal* might be the most rewarding. . . . It has been called the pivot on which European poetry of the nineteenth century turns towards the future, but it also enriches themes familiar through centuries of tradition by its own intensely individual variations. It is not as the first poet ever to discover the life of the modern city, decay, perversity or the theory of the *Correspondances* that Baudelaire matters. He creates a new kind of poetry because of his particularly penetrating insight into central human struggles and his mastery of the art of suggestion.
>
> (Alison Fairlie, *Les Fleurs du Mal*, pp. 7, 8).

If we ask why so many people have found Baudelaire to be a unique poet, the answer may be that until he wrote, poems could be thought of as beautiful words about beautiful things. He discovered a way of suggesting beauty in ugly or evil things. The beauty lacking in the object he finds in the beholder. 'Contrary to his contemporaries he did not consider that there existed any beauty in nature until the artist had put it there by seeing its significance'. (Enid Starkie, *Baudelaire*, 2nd ed. 1957, p. 531).

This need not be a conscious or logical procedure. In some cases it looks more like a game. The sonnet called *Harmonie du Soir* is not a picture of a nice evening. It is a set of four quatrains constructed on two rhymes only: soir, encensoir, reposoir, ostensoir, and tige, fige, afflige, vertige, vestige. This is the new thing, that a poet will trust to his rhyme to see what it will induce him to say, not as a means of embellishing what he knows he wants to say. Here one of his successors, Paul Valéry, is the interpreter:

> Il y a bien plus de chances pour qu'une rime procure une idée que pour trouver la rime à partir de l'idée.

It was the French Symbolist poets who drew out the implications of this new attitude to poetry. The most remarkable, a wonder poet who died before he was twenty, described poetry as a visionary activity:

> Car JE est un autre. Si le cuivre s'éveille clairon, il n'y a rien de sa faute. Cela m'est évident, j'assiste à l'éclosion de ma pensée; je la regarde, je l'écoute: je lance un coup d'archet: la symphonie fait son remuement dans les profondeurs, ou vient d'un bond sur la scène. (*Anthology of Modern French Poetry*, ed. Hackett, p. xviii).

The poet (Rimbaud) expressed himself still more cogently in a letter: 'C'est faux de dire: Je pense. On devrait dire: on me pense'.

The master and centre of the movement was a reticent self-effacing man, Stéphane Mallarmé, who took, says Mr Symons, for his principle: 'that to name is to destroy, to suggest is to create.' In his poetry 'description is banished, that beautiful things may be evoked, magically.' His own output was slim but the work of scholars upon it has been immense, an involuntary testimony to the fact that he is being regarded as a great force in modern writing. He seems to have had a quite new insight into the possibilities of language in the hands of the poet. This had better be given in his own words:

Nommer un objet, c'est supprimer les trois quarts de
la jouissance du poème qui est faite du bonheur de
deviner peu à peu; le *suggérer*, voilà le rêve. (cit.
Hackett, op. cit. p. xxiv).

He thus tried, as he said in a famous poem, to

Donner un sens plus pur aux mots de la tribu.

I do not think that the inspiration of this 'new direction'
is even yet exhausted, but it is for the young to say
whether the flood of French poetry in this century is
really pursuing new ways.

French poetry is a far more complex achievement than
this skeleton chapter can suggest. I would not like to
leave readers with the impression that the Symbolists
were moving towards a poetry so pure that it would be
divorced from life. A reminder of the way in which their
greatest disciple ended a famous poem may redress the
balance. Here is the final strophe of Paul Valéry's
Cimetière Marin:

Le vent se lève! . . . il faut tenter de vivre!
L'air immense ouvre et referme mon livre,
La vague en poudre ose jaillir des rocs!
Envolez-vous, pages tout éblouies!
   Rompez, vagues! Rompez d'eaux réjouies
Ce toit tranquille où picoraient des focs.

12 Satire

ONE WOULD THINK the French genius well suited to satire. Yet a history of French literature will contain few names of satirists. Apart from La Bruyère, no counterpart to Dryden or Pope or Swift. This is partly because few French writers have confined themselves to satire. There is a strong satiric vein in Pascal, as in Voltaire. There is satire in Molière, even in Racine, but one would not call any of these chiefly a satirist. If a French schoolboy were asked about this he would probably answer Boileau, and no less a judge than Dryden would agree with him:

> If I could only cross the seas, I might find in France a living Horace and a Juvenal, in the person of the admirable Boileau, whose numbers are excellent, whose expressions are noble, whose thoughts are just, whose language is pure, whose satire is pointed, whose sense is close . . .

The satire may have been pointed but there was not much of Juvenal about it. Boileau did indeed attack flatterers and sycophants, but he confined himself to fashion, and found his true bent in attacking bad writing. In one of his early satires, which he wrote as a paid hack, he admitted this:

> Mais dès qu'il faut railler, j'ai ce que je souhaite
> Alors, certes alors, je me reconnais poète. . . .
> Souvent j'habille en vers une maligne prose
> C'est par là que je vaux, si je vaux quelque chose.

The *Art Poétique*, which made him famous, if not in his lifetime, at least for later generations, is really a satire, to which are added hints for good writing. It was composed as a salon entertainment, and Mme de Sévigné in several letters tells of the pleasure it gave to guests at a supper party. But by Pope's time it had become a code and a theory of classical writing. In California one can see Pope's own copy bought for eightpence, in which he has neatly noted in pencil the gist of Boileau's 'precepts'. All this is a pity. It has caused schoolboys hours of drudgery and given a wrong notion of French classicism to the world. In his old age Boileau fostered the idea that a few friends had worked out together the principles of classical drama. One has only to read the first version of Satire II restored to its original text by Professor Adam, and written in 1663 when Boileau had not yet met Molière, to see how things really happened.

Taken as a satire *l'Art Poétique* is an excellent work, witty, acute, the first European assertion of the rights of criticism and of the joy of saying that bad writing is bad:

> Insipides plaisants, bouffons infortunés
> D'un jeu de mots grossier partisans surannés

It is an excellent summary of the best French taste of 1670, worked out in almost every case by showing up pretentious and feeble and pompous handling of literary form. It counsels only where it has attacked; most of the targets are not only recognisable, it is due to Boileau that they are remembered at all.

Boileau admired Pascal and especially *Les Provinciales*, possibly because it was a finer satire than he ever brought off. This masterly work, which started out as ridiculing a theological quarrel and turned into a moral indictment, was so brilliant and witty that it seems to incorporate the very genius of satire. Satire is literature of attack. 'It is the mark of the satirist that he cannot accept and refuses to tolerate' (J. Sutherland, *English Satire*, p. 4). Pascal seems to me the most intolerant of satirists. He gets nearer than any of his countrymen to the 'facit indignatio versum' of Juvenal. His attack indeed was all too successful. It gave a new connotation to the word 'jésuite', which is still in the dictionaries. It provoked no comparable literary reply but probably enflamed the opponents so much that they determined to crush Port-Royal, and did so, with Royal support. It is still a dangerous book. In Taine's day it could not be put in the catalogue of the Ecole Normale library, and in ours it cannot be set for French university examinations.

How was this achieved? As we have already seen, by a new style of writing, pungent, staccato, withering. In the early letters by the comic use of a supposed outsider seeking information. He tries to get from opposing experts the plain sense of words like 'prochain' and 'suffisant', plays one Docteur off against another to the discredit of both and to the reader's delight: after he has exposed the disagreement of the experts he gets them to say that a layman cannot grasp these things (which was not far from being the case):

Tout beau, me dit-il, il faut être Théologien pour en
voir le fin. La différence qui est entre nous est si
subtile qu'à peine pouvons-nous la marquer nous-
mêmes; vous auriez trop de difficulté à l'entendre.

We can now see that satire so sharp cuts both ways. The
real victim in the discussion is not the Jesuits but
theology itself.

If in the interests of one party you discredit the whole
debate then you no longer win. You succeed too well,
and if words are shown to be meaningless then why take
sides at all? Pascal here paves the way for Renan and
Marx.

Satire in Pascal, as in many other French writers,
shades into something else. Mr Sutherland says this also
of English satire:

Some works are satirical throughout; in others the
satire is only intermittent, one element in a more
complex effect. The lines that separate the satirical
from the unsatirical are often hard to define, either
because the writer shifts easily and rapidly from one
mood to another, or because the satirical tone is so
rarefied as to be almost imperceptible. (op. cit. p. 2).

There is satire in Molière, but *Tartuffe* is not a satire.
There is satire in Flaubert and in Proust but these
writers are clearly novelists. Satire in much modern
literature in fact must not be looked for as a genre:
it is often an ingredient in a picture of a society.

Satire in the pure state is perhaps best found in French
in the single masterpiece of La Bruyère. These *Caractères*
have really no other *raison d'être* than satiric. We are
shown pictures, of human aberrations, of people whose
power or money has gone to their heads so that they are

no longer fully human. There is the picture of the man who has dined so well that he can sign an order depriving a province of bread without realising what it means to starve. This is not realism, but exaggeration, caricature, in which every word enforces a sting. His most brilliant pictures have an emotional point which adds to the effect. What marvellous words are these:

> Ce palais, ces meubles, ces jardins, ces belles eaux, vous enchantent et vous font récrier d'une première vue sur une maison si délicieuse, et sur l'extrême bonheur du maître qui la possède. Il n'est plus, il n'en a pas joui si agréablement ni si tranquillement; il n'y a jamais eu un jour serein, ni une nuit tranquille; il s'est noyé de dettes pour la porter à ce degré de beauté où elle vous ravit. Ses créanciers l'en ont chassé; il a tourné la tête, et il l'a regardée de loin une dernière fois; et il est mort de saisissement. (VI. 79).

It is just possible that we can put our hand on the raw material of this gem of satire. It is related of Fouquet that on his way to imprisonment he was driven past a magnificent property which he had neither paid for nor ever inhabited. But how much more appealing than this reality is the perfectly rounded satiric vignette.

Nobody could deny to Voltaire the satiric gift, among so many others that decorate his work. His writings are full of attack, of brilliant irony, of positions made absurd, of mockery. *Zadig* and other philosophical tales have all these and still give pleasure. The beautiful picture of the learned men writing many volumes on the griffin, before verifying that such a creature did exist in fact, may stand for many others. The gift is used in perfection in *Candide*, one of the great French books, which should be read as a whole rather than by snippet quotations. But can this be bettered?

> A propos, dit Candide, pensez-vous que la terre ait été originairement une mer, comme on l'assure dans ce gros livre qui appartient au capitaine du vaisseau? — Je n'en crois rien du tout, dit Martin.
> . . . Mais à quelle fin ce monde a-t-il donc été formé? dit Candide. — Pour nous faire enrager, répondit Martin. . . . Croyez-vous, dit Martin, que les éperviers aient toujours mangé des pigeons quand ils en ont trouvé? — Oui, sans doute, dit Candide. — Eh bien, dit Martin, si les éperviers ont toujours eu le même caractère, pourquoi voulez-vous que les hommes aient changé le leur? — Oh, dit Candide, il y a bien de la différence, car le libre arbitre. . . . En raisonnant ainsi, ils arrivèrent à Bordeaux.

If you have a strict definition of satire, you will exclude this passage. Nobody is directly attacked in it, comedy makes part of its charm, as does a fantasy which it is difficult to define. But in a large sense one may say that in these delightful interchanges an entire way of life is put in the dock, an attitude is mocked, an evil thing is suggested. Voltaire, as Flaubert reminds us, did not find the temper of his age amusing. But the suggestion of evil is given so perfectly paradoxical a form that the reader is fascinated and won over.

There is satire in Rousseau, in de Maistre, even in Balzac, in Vigny, in Musset, and of course in their progenitor, Chateaubriand. I find it strange that French literature has no great satire of Napoleon. Mme de Staël, who alongside Chateaubriand was his chief enemy, had not the gift of satire. Nor I think had Sainte-Beuve, but the vein is rich in Flaubert. Bournisien is a terrible caricature (no doubt all too true) of a parish priest. Homais seems to me a satiric figure of large proportions, suggesting neither the middle class, nor stupidity, but something else. He is not stupid, and it would be an insult to think of Flaubert's large circle of middle-class acquaintances as copied in him. He is, to the life, the self-confident small-town philistine, keen to show learning and 'public spirit', keen above all on progress and on being associated with it. Yet in fact with no education, no sense of proportion or of human dignity, just a vast vanity. That such a man should receive a state decoration is a scandal. And a fitting end to a picture of an age.

Flaubert's best satire is a torso, elaborately prepared over the years, as the rough drafts show, but his failing powers were not equal to the task of giving it artistic form and order. He never wrote the second part of *Bouvard et Pécuchet* into which it seems he intended to put the notes on clichés and current speech, the 'sottisier' or manual of fatuity and the *Dictionnaire des Idées Reçues*, which has had some success as a separate publication and which is said to represent his hatred of all that was bourgeois.

This common opinion would seem to me unfair, to the artist no less than to the man Flaubert. He was not only an angry man; he had the ability to show the absurdity of modern fashion. He once called stupidity (la bêtise) the only enemy, and added

Je m'acharne là-dessus dans la mesure de mes moyens.

But precisely, his means were those of artistic exposure, by ridicule. Hatred is not the chief ingredient. He is nearer to Molière than to Juvenal.

The best way into his famous Dictionnaire is to read a page of notes which he called 'Catalogue des Idées chic', in which he seems to have meditated on a passage from Rousseau's *Emile* to the effect that

> il est de la dernière évidence que les compagnies savantes de l'Europe ne sont que des écoles publiques de mensonges . . .

and proceeds to suggest the kind of view which society conversation encouraged. The brief notes have an eloquence of their own when assembled. Here are a few:

> Défense de l'esclavage — De la Saint-Barthélemy — se moquer des études classiques — Dire à propos d'un grand Homme: Il est bien surfait. — Tous les grands hommes sont surfaits. Et d'ailleurs il n'y a pas de grands hommes. — Admiration de M. de Maistre . . . Science superficielle de Voltaire . . . Molière, tapissier des lettres . . . Homère n'a jamais existé. — Shakespeare n'a jamais existé, c'est Bacon qui est l'auteur de ses pièces.

If now one opens the Dictionnaire, one is in the same world of frightened sham culture:

> Abélard. Inutile d'avoir la moindre idée de sa philosophie, ni même de connaître le titre de ses ouvrages.
> Faire une allusion discrète à la mutilation opérée sur lui par Fulbert.
> Tombeau d'Héloise et d'Abélard: si l'on vous prouve qu'il est faux, s'écrier: Vous m'ôtez mes illusions.

Imagine a whole alphabet of notes of this kind. Even their assembling makes not only a great comic gallery but a satire of some weight. But again, not a satire of individuals or types, the satiric image of a way of life.

H

Let us not miss the fact that the haphazard arrangement works in favour of the satiric impression. For example:

> Peur. Donne des ailes.
> Phaeton. Inventeur des voitures de ce nom.
> Phénix. Beau nom pour une compagnie d'assurances contre l'incendie.

Or this:

> Temps. Eternel sujet de conversation.
>   Cause universelle des maladies.
>   Toujours s'en plaindre.
> Terre. Dire 'les quatre coins de la terre' puisqu'elle est ronde.
> Thème. Au collège prouve l'application, comme la version prouve l'intelligence. Mais dans le monde il faut rire des forts en thème.

It takes a great writer to impart to such formless notes a distinct sense of form. And with Flaubert this often occurs: the object is seen in contrast, a contrast so sharp with normality that it need not be made explicit in words. All that the artist need do is to suggest that 'this is the way people who claim to be intelligent individuals actually speak. This is the bondage to which apparently free modern middle-class people submit'. The bondage is clear, the norm and the aberration are set before us; the comic genius is present, through satire.

Proust must have thought of himself as a disciple of Flaubert and brings him into a satiric passage in his own great work. The lady who considered herself 'forte en littérature' asks Marcel 'comment s'appelle donc cet auteur qui a écrit *Salammbô*?' and the answer is delicious:

> Flaubert, finis-je par dire, mais le signe d'assenti-ment que fit la tête du prince étouffa le son de ma

> réponse, de sorte que mon interlocutrice ne sut pas
> exactement si j'avais dit Paul Bert ou Fulbert, noms
> qui ne lui donnèrent pas une entière satisfaction.

It would need much space to evaluate in any scholarly
manner the nature of Proust's satire. As this book is only
a pointer to literary discovery, not much need be said
here of a technical nature. On the whole, while apprecia-
ting Mr Painter's two volumes, I cannot find it in me to
agree with his judgment that Proust wrote the 'obituary
of the French nobility . . . the glory of their sunset . . .
the last social culture that our world has seen'. For this
society is exposed by the very method of the portraiture.
It is exposed as narrow, ignorant and above all snobbish.
Within its borders fashion has become a tyranny, capri-
cious in its favours, cruel in its dismissal. Swann is
welcomed so long as it suits the hostess of a particular
clan, he is banished at her whim. Near the end of the
book is a vignette of Mme Verdurin, this arbiter of social
destiny who is herself a climber. We see her faced with a
major atrocity of the first war:

(I give the original text, leaving those who are
interested to compare the excellent translation of Mr
Hudson).

> Mme Verdurin, souffrant pour ses migraines de
> ne plus avoir de croissant à tremper dans son café au
> lait, avait fini par obtenir de Cottard une ordonnance
> qui lui permit de s'en faire faire dans certain
> restaurant dont nous avons parlé. Cela avait été
> presque aussi difficile à obtenir des pouvoirs publics
> que la nomination d'un général. Elle reprit son
> premier croissant le matin où les journaux narraient
> le naufrage du *Lusitania*. Tout en trempant le
> croissant dans le café au lait, et donnant des

pichenettes à son journal pour qu'il pût se tenir grand
ouvert sans qu'elle eût besoin de détourner son autre
main des trempettes, elle disait: 'Quelle horreur.
Cela dépasse en horreur les plus affreuses tragédies'.
Mais la mort de tous ces noyés ne devait lui apparaître
que réduite au milliardième, car tout en faisant, la
bouche pleine, ces réflexions désolées, l'air qui
surnageait sur sa figure, amené là probablement par
la saveur du croissant, si précieux contre la migraine,
était plutôt celui d'une douce satisfaction.

(Pl. III. 772).

In certain books of the novel, the satiric attitude is
dominant, in *Guermantes* and in *Le Temps Retrouvé*. The
picture of the homosexual for instance may be thought of
as satiric, not of the sufferer but of the society that
makes him an outcast for living according to his nature.

There is nothing surprising in all this. Satire flourished
under the Third Republic, not only in magazines and
ephemeral plays but more sharply in the eddies and
currents of the Dreyfus Affair, most notably perhaps in
L'Ile des Pingouins of Anatole France. One senses a French
return to Swift in these mordant pages, which are more
clearly satire than they are fiction, since they do not
interest those who have no concern with their political
background. But the birds who take on human form and
repeat modern French history have now lost much of their
attraction. Only the mockery of democracy and militarism survives. In *Crainquebille*, a more accessible and
human book, the satire of urban society is tinged with
pity and humour: the attack is not so effective.

Perhaps the finest French satirist of this century is a
writer sometimes called unreadable. Charles Péguy was
many things in the short span before he met his death in

the Battle of the Marne in 1914, socialist, printer, poet, mystic, publisher, but I am persuaded that he was also a great satirist. His famous *Cahiers de la Quinzaine*, printed on the doorstep of the Sorbonne, contain the most ferocious attack which that venerable institution has ever faced. This working-class boy takes on the priests and princes of French secular culture; he mocks at a journalist who thought to 'dispose' of Joan of Arc's voices:

> Le fond de la pensée de M. Laudet, disons-le sans fard, c'est que ceux qui croient sont des imbéciles. C'est que de croire, c'est bon pour des gens comme nous autres. . . . Mais un grand seigneur, mais un grand, mais un haut esprit comme lui. . . . Pensez donc, le directeur de la Revue hebdomadaire, M. Laudet lui-même. . . .

These are new accents; they are not, and never were, read by a large public, because they are immersed in a flood of invective, and a packed breathless style that dispenses with paragraphs and seems to despise literary form. But in the midst of all this, an incisiveness, a hard-hitting invective, a pungency, that are a delight, unless one is oneself the victim. Read the page in *L'Argent* describing Lanson's lectures on Corneille at the Ecole Normale, with its mockery of the professor who knows everything except the essential, of his perfect delivery, his imperturbable manner, his omniscient and indulgent tone, until he comes up against something that he cannot measure, genius, for which one needs no learning but some humanity to grasp:

> Alors c'était Corneille. Cette fois on y était. On savait de quoi on parlait. Alors, c'était lui, Corneille . . . tout le monde avait compris que celui qui

comprend mieux *Le Cid* c'est celui qui prend *Le Cid* au ras du texte ... et surtout celui qui ne sait pas l'histoire du théâtre français. (*L'Argent*, p. 95).

Péguy has the satirist's mark of being unfair. His attacks on my own revered master of French literature, who happened to be Lanson's favourite pupil, are scandalous in their injustice. But brilliant, employing every device of rhetoric to discredit, expose, laugh out of court what Péguy considered to be a privileged and pedantic caste. With this writer one has the impression of reading and recovering an element too long absent from French satire. Mockery of the Church, of money, of wire-pulling, this the Middle Ages could show no less than La Bruyère and Voltaire. But mockery of the agnostic, the intellectual who prides himself on his freedom from belief, mockery of intellect allied to power, this only Péguy can give, and does give. The duel between Lanson and Péguy is a class war and a microcosm of antagonisms deep in French life. Curiously enough it was Lanson who in his History of French literature had pointed out as a French trait the tendency 'à railler toujours l'autorité pour manifester l'indépendance de son esprit'.

13 Tragedy

IT IS FORTUNATE that the alphabet leads us last to one of
the most impressive of French achievements in literature.
I know that this is not the general view in Anglo-Saxon
countries. The British schoolboy, to take only one
undistinguished example, does not naturally think this
way. He finds French drama cold and artificial beside
Shakespeare. He is put off, rather than attracted, by the
conventions on which it rests. Perhaps therefore it is
one of the specific tasks of universities, and of extra-
mural departments, to do something which may dispel
such misconceptions, and first of all to record the fact
that when students do take French drama seriously, to be
enjoyed on its own terms and not as a poor attempt at
English drama, then they do experience quite a new kind
of enjoyment.

It may be that Mr George Steiner is right, and that
French drama is not for export: 'the wine will not carry'.
But the wine did carry, at the start. In 1667, the year of
Andromaque, Dryden's *Essay of Dramatic Poesy* carried
an explanatory foreword which began in these terms:

> The drift of the ensuing discourse was chiefly to vindicate the honour of our English writers from the censure of those who unjustly prefer the French before them.

Not many readers of these pages will perhaps be in this category, of those who 'unjustly prefer the French'. Nor should they be. The real way to enjoy in this case is not to compare, nor (still worse) to think, as many do, that the theory of French classical drama must be known before the plays themselves can be enjoyed. Why not proceed as the scientists do in studying any new phenomenon, that is by studying the actual conditions? In the study of drama this means knowing the public which first took pleasure in the plays, noting the evidence given by the authors of how they tried to please their public; then, and only then, should we note, if we wish, the conventions which both authors and public agreed to observe. And finally take the plays, just that, take what they have to offer, unconcerned whether it is like what we are used to, or what critics have said should or should not be. This seems to me to be a scientific way of proceeding. And it is not the usual way. Take any school or university edition of the plays and see what the editor thinks we should know: you will find the life and works of the author listed and described, perhaps also the kind of play, but you will hardly ever find the aesthetic enjoyment of the play made easier for the beginner. We have a long way to go in improving the tools with which we work.

The subject is of course as technical as any other, but it is not necessary to be a scholar in order to enjoy the plays. If we do happen to be interested in unravelling what happened, we shall read learned works about the sources, the performances, the theatres, the actors, and even the authors. I do not wish to decry any of these. But my own experience is that two of the most obvious problems about the drama have hardly been investigated as yet in a modern manner, or with any satisfactory results. Nobody can tell us how or why this kind of play came to be so brilliantly written in mid-17th century. Most books suggest that it was an idea of the Pléiade poets in the Renaissance to revive the serious play in verse, and that they took Seneca as their chief model. But why should they have done this? My own guess is that the first attempts at serious drama in verse were ecclesiastical, the work of monks in the 13th century, and were not specially copied from Seneca. But that is scholars' argument. An even more pressing problem is the study of what was precisely the tragic heart of these plays, in other words what is the French idea of 'the tragic'? This too is a matter for scholars to determine, far more precisely than they have as yet done. Yet this again will dawn upon the intelligent reader as he comes to know the plays in detail and he can work out some aspects for himself.

Briefly then, what we are dealing with is a revival of serious drama according to certain conventions, a revival which may be traced back to the Pléiade, but which thanks to Richelieu receives official backing in the 1630s and which by the end of the 17th century is famous, and for the next two hundred years will remain famous, as the type of the best French theatrical art. Of the authors, the makers of these new plays, two are world figures, one might say, Pierre Corneille and Jean Racine. This enormous reputation is somewhat unfair to their contemporaries, to almost half a dozen dramatists of quality, whose plays are still worth reading if not still playable, in particular to Jean Mairet, Jean Rotrou and to

Tristan l'Hermite. Until recently these men were as neglected as the major Elizabethan dramatists apart from Shakespeare and Ben Jonson. Good modern editions have made their work accessible.

Before we deal with the poets themselves, let us be clear what the conventions were. The best known, though not the most important, were what are called the Unities, often presented as 'rules' which dramatists were forced to observe. We should rather think of them as means of heightening and concentrating interest, of cutting out deviations and digressions: a single theme, covering a restricted lapse of time, without change of place. Any play of Corneille or Racine will show how much more interest is possible if our attention be directed at one theme, and diverted by no departure from it. As a matter of fact the unities were imposed by the stagecraft of the day. A common stage direction reads: 'le théâtre s'ouvre . . .' and what was at the outset revealed stayed under the eyes of the audience until the theatrical illusion was over. The curtain was not used for separating scenes but for 'opening' and 'closing' the scenic prospect. Not knowing this, scholars have gravely discussed the rules as a tyranny which did not exist. The unities were secondary in fact to the main rule, convention, usually called *vraisemblance*, which allowed nothing on the stage but what the audience would find likely or convincing. Thus most physical action was banned because the audience would not believe it. Putting out Gloucester's eyes would have been impossible in a French 17th-century theatre because it would have been incredible. Dryden is a useful witness as to the absurdity of death on stage. 'I have observed' (says Lisideus, one of the protagonists in the *Essay*), 'that in all our tragedies the audience cannot forbear laughing, when the actors are to die: 'tis the most comic part of the whole play. . . . When we see death represented we are convinced that it is but fiction, but when we hear it related, our eyes, the strongest witnesses, are wanting, which might have undeceived us, and we are willing to favour the sleight, when the poet does not too grossly impose upon us.'

If we add to *vraisemblance* the companion quality of *bienséance*, or as we should call it, that level of elegance and propriety which never allows the artistic illusion to seem too gross or too like life, then we shall have present to our minds the pillars on which French classical tragedy is raised. It is a type of drama in which the physical illusion of actual existence is much less than in English drama, barely enough in fact to convey the illusion that it is a certain great personage, in a particular situation who is speaking, to that situation. The stress is not on realism but on intensity. To this peculiar kind of dramatic tension all the elements contribute: the grand language, the rhythm, the rhyme, the conflict of interest and of motive, rather than that of physical clash, the thorough discussion of opposing points of view, the clash of character, the progressive tightening of events so as to force unpleasant decisions on unwilling characters; above all, in and through it all, the pursuit of a single issue to its intellectual culmination. What Dryden said of classical comedy has its counterpart in tragedy: 'the greatest pleasure of the audience is a chase of wit, kept up on both sides, and swiftly managed'.

If this new kind of drama had been as dull as we in England have said, it would never have secured such a hold on the middle and upper classes of France. For the French have all the qualities needed for good theatre: they are lively, impulsive, keen, witty, intelligent, logical, and above all mad on drama. To watch an actor such as Louis Jouvet or Jean Vilar giving a modern rendering of classical drama is to realise, more keenly than by any argument, what power is still latent in this form of dramatic art.

We may admit that in mid-17th century the local conditions were favourable to drama in Paris . . . even though Molière was put to desperate straits to keep his company alive. Yet the victory of classical drama over successive generations was no accident. It might be nearer the truth to call it the work of a single man. Pierre Corneille worked for the theatre for forty-five years. After a series of pleasant verse comedies he came to serious drama, so-called, with *Médée*, and with the ever memorable *Le Cid* (1637) he came to the peak of a dramatic achievement which few authors have equalled. He was called 'le grand Corneille', said Voltaire, not to distinguish him from his brother (also a playwright) but from all other men. The enthusiasm evoked by his plays, on the most different audiences as on the most differing critics, has been enormous. Writers as different as Mme de Sévigné, Voltaire, Péguy, Schlumberger have joined in his praise. His detractors, as he more than once complained, have been many, but of his services to classical drama there can really be no doubt. I do not see how Lanson's judgment can be upset:

> Avant lui notre théâtre classique n'existait pas; par lui, il a existé.

In play after play he offered situations of intense emotion, subtle and violent, intellectual and irrational, and in doing this over a span of years he did two things of immense importance. First, he trained a public to appreciate rhetorical drama, rhetorical in all senses, drama in which ranting was frequent but not more so than real eloquence, drama in which issues of social complexity were fought out, in words, in fine words, in words that have survived the 17th-century conventions in which they arose.

Rome n'est plus dans Rome, elle est toute où je suis.

Such a line has come in France to express an attitude, but to put it so is less than the truth. It gives so fine an expression of an attitude that it may be called sublime, so pregnant in its form that a 20th-century dramatist has taken its first hemistich for his title.

But Corneille did more than train a public: he perfected a form. Why has no scholar studied the role of chance in art? It must be one of the luckiest breaks in Western literature that the form of French classical tragedy was moulded into perfection by Pierre Corneille just in time for it to serve one of the great tragic poets of the world. Racine does not alter the form; he accepts it. Perhaps we should say that he accepted it gratefully; his thoughts on the subject are not known but I have always felt that the polemic he is said to have conducted against Corneille was, if authentic, that of a young man 'on the make', in a narrow field of intense competition, and that many a time in private he must have been thankful to find a formal instrument of such delicacy and elasticity sharpened for his use.

To say that French classical tragedy is unthinkable without Corneille is not to say that he was himself a great tragic poet. For some indeed his plays are not tragic at all, and no less a person than Samuel Pepys found in them no tragic force. I do not myself see how *Le Cid* can be properly called a tragedy. Its ending is a happy reconciliation of two people who never felt anything but love for each other. But it is significant that a play which in 1637 was described as 'tragi-comédie' was in 1648, when it formed part of the first collected edition of Corneille's works, called 'tragédie'. This suggests that the mark of a tragedy was not death of the main character but something else. What could that be? Surely the tone and temper of the whole play, involving issues of life and death, having at its centre a risk of some magnitude. Corneille himself was later to say that

> l'unité d'action consiste dans la tragédie en l'unité de péril, soit que son héros y succombe, soit qu'il en sorte.

In this sense a play like *Cinna* is a tragedy. It has certainly been treated as such in France, but no less certainly it raises the question whether Corneille is any more than a powerful dramatist. Does he portray that kind of dignity in disaster which we find in Sophocles and Shakespeare and Racine? I myself could point to only two plays in which he does this. The first of these is *Horace*. The story of this famous play can be read in Livy, concerning the choice of three members of one Roman family to fight in single combat against three members of an Alban family. Horatius, the sole survivor, is met as he returns in triumph by his sister whose lover he has killed: 'The triumphant soldier was so enraged by his sister's outburst of grief in the midst of his own triumph and the public rejoicing that he drew his sword and stabbed the girl.' One can almost feel the attraction of such a subject at a time when a nation is at war, as

France was in 1640. Indeed Corneille's play has been called a study of a family in wartime. More rigorously we might call it a study of varying attitudes to war within a family. Incidentally it is a study of the ethos of militarism. What in Livy was a purple passage, the fight, is omitted by Corneille, a clear sign that he is not keen to retell the *story* of the Horatii. He is interested in the issues which confront those who must fight, in courage, in patriotism, in humanity, in pacifism. The father is a patriot, the son is a fire-eater, the opponent is a humanitarian and the sister and wife both hate war as destructive of the family. The sister is made of the same stuff as her brother, equally fanatical, and her defiance of him has not only made her role one of the most famous in theatrical history; it has provided a test piece for the aspirant to the stage. It should be not only read, but declaimed, and compared with a contemporary English translation. There is no time like the present. This is what English audiences read, and possibly heard, in 1665:

> Rome, that alone does my affliction prove!
> Rome, to whom thou hast sacrificed my love!
> Rome that first gave thee life, that perfectly
> I hate because she does so honour thee!
> May all her neighbours in one cause conspire
> To sack her walls and ruin her by Fire!
> And if all Italy appear too few
> May East and West join in the mischief too
> Far as the frozen poles may Nations come
> O'er hills and seas to sack imperious Rome!

Put this back in a 17th-century theatrical atmosphere and you have a certain grandeur, which lay in the skill of the actor to realise. Make allowances for the servitudes of translation and you may conjecture that the original was moving and exalting in a far more persuasively rhetorical way. As indeed it still may be:

> Rome, l'unique objet de mon ressentiment!
> Rome, à qui vient ton bras d'immoler mon amant!
> Rome qui t'a vu naître, et que ton coeur adore!
> Rome enfin que je hais parce qu'elle t'honore!
> Puissent tous ses voisins ensemble conjurés
> Saper ses fondements encor mal assurés!
> Et si ce n'est assez à toute l'Italie,
> Que l'Orient contre elle à l'Occident s'allie;
> Que cent peuples unis des bouts de l'univers
> Passent pour la détruire et les monts et les mers!
> Qu'elle-même sur soi renverse ses murailles,
> Et de ses propres mains déchire ses entrailles!
> Que le courroux du ciel allumé par mes voeux
> Fasse pleuvoir sur elle un déluge de feux!
> Puissé-je de mes yeux y voir tomber ce foudre,
> Voir ses maisons en cendre, et tes lauriers en poudre,
> Voir le dernier Romain à son dernier soupir,
> Moi seule en être cause, et mourir de plaisir!
>
> (iv. 5).

In calling this a purple passage I do not mean that it should be read or appreciated in isolation. It does not stand by itself as an eloquent exception; it is in the body of the play, it suggests the cause of the tragedy; in form it is traditional and artificial. We must not imagine that anyone ever actually said this; the criterion of realism is out of place here. Ancient drama frequently ended with a curse or a pronouncement of doom pronounced by the personage condemned to die. The poet modernises this element and makes it contribute to an ideal expression of all that can be said and suggested against military tyranny. Camille, the speaker, is indeed the feminist and the pacifist; her role is to suggest, in terms that are powerful precisely because they are artificial and rhetorical, the eternal protest of outraged humanity against war and the military mind. The speech is thus part of a discussion; it enforces a point and contributes to the tragic heart and centre of the action. I know no more tragic picture of the demon of militarism than this play. The role of the soldier in society is more adequately seized by Corneille than it will be even by Vigny in his famous stories of *Servitude et Grandeur Militaires*. The soldier is essential to the community; he saves the state by his unquestioning and fearless obedience. But this hard quality of iron resolution is double-edged; it allows the soldier to blur the distinction between war and murder. The play even suggests that there may be no such distinction. *Horace* is a poignant tragedy, a tragedy of fanaticism, Corneille's favourite theme. It suggests demonic forces at work in the very textures of our society. Surely here is tragedy, authentic, modern.

Polyeucte (1644) is a more difficult play and interpretations sharply diverge. Its theme is martyrdom and this is in itself not tragic since the victim desires death. The tragic aspect comes in with the peculiar character of the martyr, again a fanatic like Horace. He will brook no compromise and no delay; he has all the enthusiasm of a recent convert. His cruel disregard of his wife indeed borrows the very language of Horace:

Je ne vous connais plus si vous n'êtes chrétienne.

Pauline is indeed in the very centre of the action, caught between her duty to a husband anxious to be rid of her and her inclination for a past lover whose political power affects all the characters. The play has beautiful lines and

I

conveys a sense of the tragic possibilities of fanaticism even (perhaps most of all) in religion.

These are in many ways Racinian conflicts but Jean Racine, with greater poetic power, seems to use the classical form created by Corneille to its maximum effect. His greatest skill is to show a group of people doomed to death or failure because of their selfish nature. In *Andromaque* for instance (1667), one of the world's great plays, of the four main characters, an ambassador, a conqueror, a captive queen and a princess, one goes mad, one is murdered, one commits suicide, leaving only one, the captive queen, alive. In *Britannicus* we are shown a superb study of the young Nero, not so much wicked as weak, prevented from adult independence by his hectoring mother, almost bullied into crime, one might say. But for the bluster of Agrippine, the good counsellor might prevail over the wicked counsellor. But the latter has always the trump card: if you go straight, they will say it is mother who still rules. This kind of tragedy uses the Cornelian form to attain ends and effects which Corneille never contemplated.

Racine's dramatic career was meteoric, all over before he was forty. Yet with each play he achieved a fresh kind of tragic effect. In *Bérénice* he shows the conflicting claims of love and duty, forcing the Emperor to part with the Queen and thus to ruin both their lives. This is so clear that nothing but the actual parting is needed for the full tragic effect. As the poet said in his preface:

> Ce n'est point une nécessité qu'il y ait du sang et des morts dans une tragédie: il suffit que l'action en soit grande, que les acteurs en soient héroïques, que les passions y soient excitées, et que tout s'y ressente de cette tristesse majestueuse qui fait tout le plaisir de la tragédie.

The fourth masterpiece, *Bajazet*, is an even greater surprise. Racine achieves the tragedy of primitive passion without stressing the heroic element at all. All takes place in a harem in the master's absence. A slave offers a prince the choice of death or marriage. When he chooses death, we know that means her death also and that she is the more pitifully tragic

> Dans ma juste fureur observant le perfide,
> Je saurai le surprendre avec son Atalide;
> Et d'un même poignard les unissant tous deux,
> Les percer l'un et l'autre, et moi-même après eux.
>
> (IV. 4).

By convention these lines must on stage be spoken, but they are part of a monologue, that is of the imagined thoughts, in this case of a tortured spirit. This is the privilege of classical drama, that it can suggest the inner mind. Racine excels in devising situations where the necessity of choice, between one's pride and one's peace of mind, is agonising and would be felt as such were it not for the perfection of the verse. As an American critic has written:

> In the perfect balance of the rhymed couplet, in the perfect balance of the individual line . . . one feels the logical form of thesis and antithesis, the tragic split between reason and passion.
>
> (Fergusson, *Idea of a Theater*, p. 66).

It would take us beyond the proper limits of this chapter to trace how in five more experiments Racine again achieved tragic moments, usually in the confrontation of passionate people with an opponent or with their better nature. In *Mithridate* the struggle is between the conqueror, who can fight Rome but cannot handle a woman of dignity. In *Iphigénie* the myth shows Agamemnon faced with the choice of rescue for his ships at the price of sacrificing his own daughter. In *Phèdre* we meet with the most cosmic picture of all, embodying in a single figure the claim of conscience and the undeniable existence of passion. Not for nothing did French officers in a war prison in Silesia find in 'notre mère Phèdre' their greatest national suggestion of tragedy. It was tragedy within the *persona*, within all of us, the tragedy of being an adult person. It would need a book to explain but can be enjoyed by anyone who loves musical French and appreciates formal beauty.

A rather special type of appreciation is needed however for the final work of Racine. *Athalie* as a source of aesthetic pleasure is a sealed book for many Anglo-Saxons, partly because its theme, the tragic conflict of God and evil, is confused with its subject, the biblical story of the savage death of a usurping queen. Since the Old Testament case of Athalia was quoted in the debates about William III and the Stuart succession, it was natural for Racine to hear it discussed and his dramatic instinct led him to choose it as a subject for dramatic edification for the girls of Madame de Maintenon's school at Saint-Cyr. But the result was very different from the intention:

> ... le plus sensuel et le plus terrible des poètes écrit des tragédies pour les petites filles.
>
> (Maulnier, *Racine*, p. 255).

The first of the two tragedies of which M. Maulnier speaks, *Esther*, caused such an effect when acted by the girls that the second was ordered to be declaimed and not acted. Nevertheless it proved to be in the end, and at the end, Racine's most pitiless play. The picture left in the mind of the reprobate queen hounded by God and the Israelites to her death, and cursing her creator, is the nearest thing in French to Milton's Satan, and was said by Voltaire to be 'le chef-d'oeuvre de l'esprit humain'. It is part of the genius of Racine that he could fill a play with artifice, keeping the matter more or less true to its source in the Bible, and yet portray the human condition of passionate independence as tragic, tragic because it was doomed, for the creature could never win against the creator. Yet what grander scale can be imagined for any tragedy? 'Le sujet de Racine est la perte de l'homme' (op. cit. p. 262).

And there our survey might well end. The story is well known, and has been recently told by Mr Steiner, in *The Death of Tragedy*. The form continued to be cultivated, even by such clever poets as Voltaire, but produced no more achievements. The Enlightenment called into question the assumptions of classical tragedy. The novel has in the modern age absorbed much of the power of dramatic tragedy. 'Mes romans bourgeois sont plus tragiques que vos tragédies' said Balzac to the dramatists of his day, and such a tragedy (is it not such?) as *La Recherche de l'Absolu* would confirm his boast.

After the classical period the tragic form of drama seems to have been eclipsed in France . . . until the Romantics. Alfred de Musset's play *Lorenzaccio* seems to me to have all the ingredients of real tragedy. Even though set in 15th-century Florence it is tragedy with a modern ring. The murder done to save the state from the tyrant is not only ineffective: it leads to the death of the patriot. Lorenzo is not only in Hamlet's position; he has something of his bewilderment before human circumstance; in this play 'great enterprises . . . lose the name of action'.

An even more desperate attempt at recovery of a lost genre was made by the Symbolist poet Villiers de l'Isle Adam. His *Axel* comes nearer than any late 19th-century play to the atmosphere of the tragic, but it is a desperate throw and the effect is muted.

Conclusion

THERE IS NOT MUCH left to say. I have tried not to write a history but to describe an achievement. With the comments of those who listened to these lectures in mind let me point up the distinction.

It is a pity to equate performance and achievement. In the palace of art there are many mansions and many grades of merit. Bad art must be studied because it has often been of great influence on men of genius. Authors of all kinds and talents can claim a place in the histories of art, and of literature in particular. But much literary production does not last beyond its own age. If its power has departed there is no need to recall it, except in theses and monographs and bibliographies.

But some works of art obviously do survive their age. They give pleasure to those of later ages; they continue to have compelling power, to charm, to excite, to inspire. This is the case of *Robinson Crusoe*, while the rest of Defoe's works have had their day. Most books, like most people, die a natural death. In fact, as a French scholar has said, 'le passé littéraire, c'est quelques livres qui subsistent'. It is of such books that the achievement of a nation in literature is composed. It is of such books that these pages have tried to give some image.

The great works of a nation's literature, as I have said already, are talked of as if they belonged to one of three kinds of work. But this is to narrow unduly the scope of good writing. It consists, not only of poems, plays and novels, but of other kinds as well. What we might call literature of power, that is, books which have given great pleasure or stimulated others to re-think the world, do not happen to be poems or plays or novels. They include one or two dictionaries, some collections of epigrams, some private letters. There should be nothing surprising in this. The power to write well may emerge in a sermon as in a sonnet. The comic spirit may animate a pamphlet no less than a play. I have endeavoured not to narrow the domain of literature.

One more conclusion seems to be relevant. Many of the 'achievements' spoken of in these pages are famous works in their own right. They are so, but they are something more than that. They are items of a great debate. We might not be far out in thinking of modern literature as a single long argument, on a vast theme, no less than the nature of man. An immense commentary, one might say, on the line:

What a piece of work is a man.

The exciting thing to watch is not so much the individual contributions to the debate as the changing emphasis. In 1500—and this is what makes Renaissance writing so strange to us—books were written within a hierarchy and scale of values. These values were not seriously questioned. Man was surrounded by revelation, most of it enshrined in the Bible. The powers in his world, monarchy, nobility, knowledge, greatest of all the Church, from the archbishops down to the local curé, all these represented authority; they were to be obeyed and not questioned.

But it was just these things which during the next three hundred years were to face questions, more and more insistent and by more and more people. Authority was to produce its great figures: Richelieu and Bossuet thought that the ordinary man should submit, and not enquire. Fontenelle and Voltaire trained men to disbelieve what was handed to them on authority. Diderot, Kant and Renan and many more continued the sceptical attack, until we find a master of intelligence like Sainte-Beuve saying in 1859 that everything is open to question.

From the Renaissance onwards this spirit of criticism went hand in hand with the spirit of comedy, with wit and burlesque and mock-heroic. The style of the grand epic was parodied, even the solemn form of tragedy fell into disrepute. The creators of this new world of intelligent criticism and assessment were writers such as Erasmus, Rabelais, Cervantes, Shakespeare, Molière, Boileau. This last, greatly misunderstood even now, actually wrote a parody of epic and of the hero in fiction. So none of the works now rated as famous can be thought of in isolation. They are links in a chain of dialectic.

In our time the wheel has come full circle. The relativism of the 19th century has been overcome. Symbolism, a French movement, made a case for absolute values in poetry. Writers like Kafka and Nietzsche and Claudel suggested that reason was the servant of dark powers, some of them thought of as being outside man and some within man.

In this debate France has played a leading role. I do not claim that French literature is deeper or richer in content than any other: such claims are too individual to have much general validity. But the advantage of the French lies in their lucidity, in the capacity to formulate and to express what others have felt. This is what gives to their more successful works of literature a power of communication that surprises the reader. One may say that they are never pedantic, heavy, abstruse. One of their greatest writers, Voltaire, indeed gives the contrary impression, of treating grave matters lightly and frivolously. But *Candide* is no frivolity and French grace of writing usually covers matters of grave complexity.

Words are powerful things, but they cannot transmit the past, in anything but flashes and echoes. And I doubt whether what we find in books about the past has any great virtue in itself. Let us keep some proportion in our studies, that proportion which the French never forget, and which in a space era is essential: 'Car enfin, qu'est-ce que l'homme dans l'infini?' It is still a leading question.

Further reading suggested
by the various sections

ABBREVIATIONS:
G = Classiques Garnier. N = Nelson Collection
Pl = Editions de la Pléiade
TFM = Textes Français Modernes

1. The *Mémoires* of Retz and Saint-Simon are both
   available in Pl.
   E. Auerbach, *Mimesis. The representation of reality in
   western literature*, Doubleday paperback, 1946.
   Rousseau, *Confessions*, ed. J. Vigne Voysine, G.,
   1964.
   Chateaubriand, *Mémoires d'Outre-tombe*, ed. Levaillant,
   4 vols.
   Gide, *Journal* I and II, Pl.

2. R. Bray, *Molière, homme de théâtre*, 1954.
   Molière, critical essays, ed. J. Guicharnaud, 1964.
   Meredith, *The Idea of Comedy and the Uses of the
   Comic Spirit*, 1877.

3. Bayle, *Choix de textes*, ed. M. Raymond, 1948.
   Encyclopedia, Selected articles, ed. Lough, 1954.
   Selections, ed. Gendzier, Harper paperback, 1967.
   H. N. Brailsford, *Voltaire*, 1935. O.U.P. paperback,
   1963.
   H. T. Mason, *Pierre Bayle and Voltaire*, O.U.P., 1963.

4. Sartre, *Les Mouches*, ed. North, Harrap, 1963.
   Becque, *Les Corbeaux*, ed. Lockerbie, Harrap, 1962.

5. La Rochefoucauld, *Maximes*, ed. Secretan, TFM., 1967.

6. Montaigne, *Essais*, Pl.
   Sainte-Beuve, *Causeries du Lundi* and *Nouveaux Lundis*.
   Valéry, *Variété*, 7 vols.

7. *Extraits des historiens français du 19e siècle*, ed. Jullian, Hachette, 1908.
   E. Wilson, *To the Finland Station. A study in the writing and acting of history*, Fontana paperback.

8. Mme de Sévigné, *Lettres*, 3 vols, Pl.
   Flaubert, *Correspondance*, 9 vols, Conard.
   Voltaire, *Correspondance*, ed. Besterman, Pl.

9. Mme de La Fayette, *La Princesse de Clèves*, ed. Kettle, Univ. of London Press.
   Laclos, *Les Liaisons Dangereuses*, ed. Le Hir, G.
   Rousseau, *Julie, ou la Nouvelle Héloïse*, ed. Mornet, 4 vols.
   Stendhal, *Le Rouge et le Noir*, N.
   Zola, *Thérèse Raquin*, translated L. W. Tancock, Penguin.
   Balzac, *Short Stories*, ed. Raitt, O.U.P. The major novels in G.
   Henry James, *The Art of Fiction*, O.U.P., 1948.
   H. J. Hunt, *Balzac's Comédie Humaine*, Univ. of London Press, 1959.
   Proust, *Combray*, ed. Brée and Lynes, Harrap.

10. Flaubert, *Trois Contes*, ed. Duckworth, Harrap.
    Maupassant, *Selected Short Stories*, ed. Matthews, 1959.
    Gordon and Tate, *The House of Fiction*, Scribner's Paperback, 1960.

11. *The Poetry of France. An Anthology*, ed. A. Boase, 3 vols, Methuen, 1964.
    The Oxford Book of French Verse, revised by P. Mansell Jones, 1957.
    Anthology of Modern French Poetry, ed. C. A. Hackett, Blackwell, 1952.

12. A. Adam, *Les Premières Satires de Boileau*, Lille, 1941.
    Halévy, *Péguy et les Cahiers de la Quinzaine*, 1941.
    Charles Péguy, *Oeuvres en Prose*, Pl., 1958.
    Bernard Guyon, *Péguy*, 1960.
    G. D. Painter, *Marcel Proust, A Biography* 2 vols., Chatto, 1959, 1965.

13. G. Steiner, *The Death of Tragedy*, 1961.
    Odette de Mourgues, *Racine, or the Triumph of Relevance*, C.U.P., 1967.
    Corneille, *Horace*, ed. Moore, Blackwell, 1953.
    F. Fergusson, *The Idea of a theater*, Doubleday paperback, 1949.
    Racine, *Phédre*, ed. R. C. Knight, Manchester. U.P.